DEEP EQUALITY

LIVING IN THE FLOW
OF NATURAL RHYTHMS

Jocelyn Chaplin

BOOKS

Winchester, UK
Washington, USA

DEEP EQUALITY

LIVING IN THE FLOW
OF NATURAL RHYTHMS

First published by O Books, 2008
O Books is an imprint of John Hunt Publishing
Ltd., The Bothy, Deershot Lodge, Park Lane,
Ropley, Hants, SO24 0BE, UK
office1@o-books.net
www.o-books.net

Distribution in:

UK and Europe
Orca Book Services
orders@orcabookservices.co.uk
Tel: 01202 665432 Fax: 01202 666219 Int. code
(44)

USA and Canada
NBN
custserv@nbnbooks.com
Tel: 1 800 462 6420 Fax: 1 800 338 4550

Australia and New Zealand
Brumby Books
sales@brumbybooks.com.au
Tel: 61 3 9761 5535 Fax: 61 3 9761 7095

Far East (offices in Singapore, Thailand, Hong
Kong, Taiwan)
Pansing Distribution Pte Ltd
kemal@pansing.com
Tel: 65 6319 9939 Fax: 65 6462 5761
South Africa
Alternative Books
altbook@peterhyde.co.za
Tel: 021 555 4027 Fax: 021 447 1430

ISBN: 978 1 84694 096 5

A CIP catalogue record for this book is available
from the British Library.

Printed by Chris Fowler International
www.chrisfowler.com

Text copyright Jocelyn Chaplin 2008

Design: Stuart Davies

O Books operates a distinctive and ethical publishing philosophy in
all areas of its business, from its global network of authors to
production and worldwide distribution.
This book is produced on FSC certified stock, within ISO14001
standards. The printer plants sufficient trees each year through
the Woodland Trust to absorb the level of emitted carbon in
its production.

CONTENTS

This book is dedicated to my daughter Rosita who embodies the Spirit of Love, and to all the Ancestors and Beings who kept alive the Flow of Loving Rebellion in times of Inequality.

PREFACE

I wrote this book for people like me, who feel strongly about injustice and inequality, but also long for that deeper connection to nature's rhythms and energies, some call spirituality. Like so many, I rebelled against my parents' religion. They were missionaries in southern Sudan. But it was there in the bush, that I first remember feeling an overwhelming longing for something outside. It was something that church never satisfied, something linked to the distant drums I heard at night. There began a long journey that I am sharing in these pages, with a hope that it will inspire others.

Later experiences, as a white child in a black school in Ghana, taught me about the complexities of equality issues. I belonged to the oppressor group but also worshipped the beautiful African girls in my class. I felt inferior. I was pale and ugly. I could not dance and most importantly, I had no rhythm.

It was on the plane returning from Africa for the last time in my twenties that I first discovered the idea of rhythm as a philosophy of living. It was 1969. I was reading an interview with Jimi Hendrix in Time Magazine. The words 'Life is Rhythm' jumped out at me, and I have been researching the concept ever since. The theory that everything in the universe is rhythmic in one way or another is central to this book. For those who are interested, there are references to philosophers and scientists to follow up the more theoretical aspects. These are woven in with the more practical ones.

Back in the UK I identified with the woman's movement and had the opposite experience of being part of an oppressed group under patriarchy. Much of my early political activity and writing was around feminism, and later goddess spirituality. It seemed to me that they were both trying to dissolve all hierarchical structures, not just gender ones. I joined the Socialist Worker's Party, but became disillusioned with the left's attempts to impose equality from above. Over the last ten years I have begun to explore ways of equalizing from below, from within, out of human needs, not rigid doctrines. Through years of practice and analysis came the idea that equalizing is basically a balancing process going on in nature and in our psyches at all levels. One friend describes this book as a travel guide to Equalizing Rhythms. We can find them in the most surprising hidden corners of the world, from the smallest bits of matter to the depths of our unconscious minds, from carnival to rave culture.

But most importantly, this is a book with practical suggestions about experiencing living differently. I share techniques and examples to encourage us all to be more in the flow, to be freer, more attuned and able to balance our inner opposites. This book is for people already on a spiritual path, or not, people politically involved, or not, and people working on their personal development, or not.

Reading these pages can itself be like dancing between the opposites of the personal and the political (in the broadest sense of equalizing), between theory and practice, between the individual and the collective and between words and images. I hope it will speak to your intuition as well as to your intellect, and help 'join up the dots' between the eternal moments of Now.

ACKNOWLEDGEMENTS

I would like to thank all those clients, students and colleagues who have shared their innermost journeys with me in one way or another. Though names and details are changed, so many of the examples given in the book come from their courage and inner wisdom. I also want to mention the support given by Linda Latter, Beverley Franklin, Mary-Jane Rust, Claire Walsh, Amelie Noac, Jocelyn Wellburn, Raficq Abdulla, Beatrice Millar, Mildred Levious, my mother Joyce Chaplin and brother Nigel Chaplin. There have been many others too. But I especially thank Cliff Ashcroft for his advice and encouragement on the manuscript of this book in its early stages.

CHAPTER ONE

LIVING RHYTHMICALLY

'In the future elaboration of the new holistic world view, the notion of rhythm is likely to play a very fundamental role.' Fritjof Capra, 1982.

'Life is rhythm.' Jimi Hendrix, interview in Life magazine, August 1969.

We have all had experiences of living rhythmically, for a few minutes, a few hours, even days, tuned in to the deepest balancing needs and energies of the moment. It can be when we are in love. We may remember gliding together through the unfamiliar streets of a distant town and finding ourselves by 'chance' outside the perfect cafe for intimate conversation. It could be during a meditation retreat, slowed down in an atmosphere of inner focus. Synchronicities are happening. We find ourselves sitting next to a long lost friend on a train or seeing the very book we have been searching for fall off a shelf in a book shop we nearly did not visit. Or it could be when we are acting wholeheartedly for justice, supporting the underdog in a conflict. There is a strange feeling of 'rightness'. It is not 'right' in a moral religious sense. We could be breaking the law, trespassing on 'private' land or ignoring a religious decree. But instead of obeying an outside authority, something deep in our soul knows that we are in the right place at the right time. One popular way of describing this, is being 'in the in the flow'.

We can often feel more 'in the flow' when traveling or on holiday. Some years ago I worked as a psychotherapist with a young woman whose main issue was the conflict between dependence and independence. It was August and we were having our usual summer break. I went off to meet my Greek boyfriend in Athens. After a few days we decided to 'go with the flow' and catch the first boat to whatever island it was going. That was how we ended up in Naxos, the island of Ariadne and Dionysus. On arrival we followed the labyrinthine alleyways of the old town through shaded tunnels and ancient archways up to the top of the hill. And there in front of us was the Hotel Dionysus covered in bright purple bougainvillea and fading green shutters. There was just one room available. For many days we were lost in one another. Then one hot afternoon I left my lover sleeping to sit outside and do some sketching. I sat on one of the curving steps that wound down towards the port. Looking up from my work I saw this figure with an enormous backpack struggling up the hill towards me. As she got closer I realized to my astonishment that it was my young client. We flew into each other's arms and hugged, quite unlike the way most therapists and clients behave. She had left her friends on another island and come to Naxos on her own for the first time in her life!

And then we lose it. What is the 'it' that we lose? And how can we find it again?

Going With What Flow?

The Turkish writer Orhan Pamuk[1] put this search quite simply. 'It is as if I am looking for that special place and time in which everything flows into everything else, everything is linked and everything is aware of everything else.' Some would call it being connected to god or goddess, Allah or Great Spirit. Others of us are exploring alternative ways of describing the same kinds of experiences. It does not even have to be described as spiritual. The psychologist Daniel Goleman[2] describes the highest form of emotional intelligence as being able to be in the flow. For him this means being 'aligned with the task at hand, with a feeling of joy, even rapture.' He also notes that while in the flow, people are not concerned with thoughts of success and failure. Mihaly Csikszentmihalyi[3] writes that 'it is the full involvement of flow, rather than happiness that makes for excellence in life'.

I suggest there are seven different human states associated with being in the flow:

1. Unselfconsciousness, unconcerned with other's opinions
2. Non judging, so no ups and downs, no success or failure
3. Calm and/or joyful feelings, perhaps including a sense of streaming energy
4. No sense of ego, so no feelings of separateness
5. Being in the present moment, so no thoughts of future or past
6. Attuned intuitively to the deepest needs of the moment
7. Opposite states flow into each other organically rather than being split into competing extremes.

But how do we get there? Is it simply a passive surrender to something? Those who see this way of thinking as far too simple, remind us that 'only dead fish go with the river's flow'. Sometimes 'going with the flow' is contrasted with having clearly defined goals. But we can all find examples in our lives of having both an intention and a trust in the flow to get us there.

There does not always need to be a detailed plan or a sense of being personally totally 'in control' all the time. Such control leaves little room for other unpredictable but often significant happenings. Living rhythmically implies a balance between control and surrender, reason and intuition, living fully in the present and some sensible planning ahead. Small examples of travel, even through a few empty streets, can be useful metaphors for following the flow in the wider landscapes of our whole lives.

One wet Saturday I met a friend in the semi-deserted city of London to wander the streets together and follow the flow. We had an intention to find the Templar's church that we knew was somewhere off Fleet Street. First we connected to the spirit of St Paul's Cathedral, meditating on the Temple of Diana buried deep underneath. This put us in a kind of trance state, and coming down the hill were soon 'lost' in some old alleyways. Then to our relief we saw a newsagents still open. I went in to ask for directions. A small boy in a cloak was buying sweets. The child turned round with an angelic smile, and offered to take us to the church. Chatting on the way, it turned out that he was going to choir practice and his father just happened to be the Bishop of London! This encounter had special meaning for me, as a few years previously I had run a workshop in St James church in Piccadilly on sexuality and spirituality. The Bishop of London had complained and tried to cancel it. So we achieved our goal but something in the wider flow had also been balanced for me. These events would never have happened if we had used a street map.

Critics also imply that 'going with the flow' means there is no structure. It's true that the structure is not always immediately obvious to the naked eye, or even to modern scientific understanding. But something is going on. There does seem to be a hidden structure or form. It isn't random. This book is an exploration of one form such a structure could take. It is called the ever-changing structure of equalizing rhythms or the flow between opposites on different levels and in different dimensions. A rhythm could be described as a repeating pattern of energy flow between opposites over time. They connect sound and silence, up and down, dark and light. They are the forms taken by the rise and fall of entire civilizations and of the tides and waves of the sea. Everything is vibrating in fast or slow, super fast or super slow, repeating or varying rhythms. The form of equalizing rhythm can be described as an ever-moving structure underlying apparent structurelessness or chaos. It could be described visually as the thousands of wavy lines that pass through the various opposites. These moving structures are not circles. There is never any coming back to exactly the same place. Each time is different. These endless flowing rhythms, in many dimensions could be portrayed as multidimensional images of dancing snakes.

Clearly our attunement to the rhythmic flow – or should we say the many flows between many opposites – is complex. It is not just being

Multidimensional rhythms

fully engaged with a particular task (such a task could involve warfare or cruelty). It seems to encourage a sense of connectedness and empathy with other humans. It involves attunement to some of the mysterious bigger flows between opposites in a wider sense between 'me' and 'not me', between power and powerlessness, destruction and creation, high and low.

It seems that there are always opposites involved, but instead of these being rigidly and vertically arranged there is a rhythmic dance between them. One opposite turns into the other. Energy flows between them in different ways and on different levels. Cosmologists tell us that we still only understand five per cent of the universe with our current scientific knowledge. The rest is rather poetically called dark matter and dark energy! So however hard we try to understand these flowing rhythmic processes, our attempts are bound to be extremely limited and partial. This has not stopped philosophers and psychologists, shamans and theologians, scientists and mystics throughout history trying to understand.

Rhythmic Flow in Ancient and Modern Philosophy
The Western philosopher most associated with the flow lived in Ephesus, Turkey, in the 5th Century BC. His name was Heraclitus[4], and he spent most of his later years playing with children on the steps of the temple. Although only fragments of his writings survived, he has influenced a whole strand of philosophical thought up to the present day. He was the one who famously wrote that 'everything flows' and 'you can't step into the same river twice'.

The idea that ultimately everything is in process has become part of our modern vocabulary, especially in personal development. We talk of 'trusting the process', seeing the importance of 'the process rather than just the product'. According to the 20th Century process philosopher, AN Whitehead[5] 'the elucidation of the sentence "everything flows" is one of the main tasks for the world today'. Some even imagine the 'process' itself as a kind of divine energy. The feminist theologian Carol Christ[6] describes the divine feminine as being represented through a 'process paradigm'. She specifically refers to it as an alternative to masculine dualistic theologies. The feminine way 'affirms life while holding together both sides of the classical dualisms ... male and female etc'. So the opposites are still there but we connect them differently. There is a flow between them rather than a vertical division.

When we are in the flow, we are in a dance between the masculine and feminine. It could be in relation to another person, or between the inner masculine and feminine sides of ourselves. A friend told me that when she felt fully in the flow there was less of a desperate need to have a partner to 'dance' with. She was already in her own dance.

A female client of mine in a senior management position found herself swinging between being very bossy, even tyrannical, and completely laissez faire at work. After assertiveness training she gradually found a way of being less autocratic, but strong and clear. This actually made it easier to express her more 'feminine' ability to support her employees. It allowed a natural flow into empathetic listening to her team. She could then dance freely between the two sides.

A male client had a divide between the opposites of perfection and hopelessness. He could not fully express his creative side because he had to be perfect. Overcoming his writer's block involved allowing himself just to write anything down at a given time and not judge it. We worked for years on increasing his general self-esteem. The lower opposite of hopelessness was raised and the higher one of perfection was lowered, so that there could be a flow.

This flow between opposites is exactly what another ancient philosopher Lao Tsu[7] describes in the Chinese Tao Te Ching. 'The Tao of heaven is like the bending of a bow. The high is lowered and the low is raised. Soft and weak overcomes hard and strong.' So said Lao Tsu, in 500 BC. All the passages describe the interrelatedness of opposites and how one flows, merges and turns into the other over time. Taoism can be described as rhythmic in the sense that a rhythm is a movement in time between opposite states. It is a flow of energy forwards and backwards, to-ing and fro-ing. There is endless returning, endless rhythm, endless alternation.

A much later philosopher from the 19th Century, G W F Hegel,[8] developed a similar dialectical approach to opposites. He saw the flow between them as the spirit in matter. Engels,[9] who was determined to apply this theory to material reality, saw dialectical thought as 'only the reflection of the motion of opposites which asserts itself in nature'. As in Taoism there is a belief that human thought (or philosophy) can follow the deepest structures of nature, the rhythmic interconnection of opposites. And because one flows into the other, neither opposite can be permanently superior. There is kind of equality. The process balances and equalizes the opposites. So the form of flow can be described as equalizing rhythms. Rhythmic thinking, or the rhythmic paradigm, follows the rhythm forms that exist throughout nature. As the physicist philosopher Fritjof Capra[10] writes, 'Rhythmic patterns seem to be manifest (in nature) at all levels.'

Most people in the modern world are out of tune with their own rhythmic natures as well as those of planet earth. A client found herself working in an office culture that insisted on extremely long hours. She was exhausted and depressed. This woman had completely lost touch with her own natural rhythm of work and rest. By refusing to work the long hours and losing out on her chances of promotion, she began to feel more in tune with her own rhythms. She stayed at home a lot in the winter and became more active in the summer. She slept more hours and took short breaks every two hours at work. She used the moon cycles to attune her energy flow. New projects were started on the new moon.

In fact this concept of rhythmic flow may be the deep philosophy around which most of human life was once organized. Many ancient and native societies appear to be better attuned to nature and her many rhythms. But this model or paradigm seems to have got lost to mainstream societies in the West and East around 6,000 – 4,000 years ago when more hierarchical thinking took over.

Meanwhile, the thread of the rhythmic philosophy never completely disappeared. It was kept alive in Taoism in China, in the philosophy of Heraclitus in ancient Greece, and in the spirituality of native peoples using ideas such as the Da in Africa. 'The Da incarnates the quality of dynamics in life – movement, flexibility, sinuousness, fortune. It manifests itself as serpent, as rainbow as umbilicus ... All nature contains energy from the Da.' [11]

Talking to the Da

Rhythmic Flow in Psychological Processes

This creative process itself can be seen as the flow between opposites. As William Blake wrote, 'No progression without contraries'[12]. These opposites can be electrical positives and negatives, dark and light, up and down, joy and sorrow... ad infinitum. But the shape taken by this flow appears to be a pattern with an alternating rhythmic form. Sylvia Perera[13], a Jungian analyst writing of the 'way of the feminine', describes how the alternating paradigm was once so primary in ancient Mesopotamia, but modern 'civilization' has repressed this way of thinking and being, to the serious psychological detriment of human beings.

Jung called this equalizing process that operates in our unconscious 'enantiodromia'. It is a Greek word that can be translated as 'the way of opposites'. When one opposite is reached there is a natural swing back to the other side. We are constantly trying to rebalance our imbalanced inner sides. Examples that Jung uses include our light and shadow sides, our masculine and feminine sides and our feeling and thinking sides. Neither side is superior. The emotionally intelligent or individuating person is able to equalize the opposites over time.

In our human world the drive to equalize can be seen as the equivalent of the balancing force in nature. This equalizing rhythmic structure that underlies the flow gives us different ways of thinking, different paradigms to apply in everyday life. If we started to think rhythmically it would involve a complete shift in the very basic structure of our consciousness. Such a transformation involves going to the very roots of our thinking processes, and it could be just the kind of radical change that the world desperately needs for the 21st Century.

'*With the splitting of the atom everything has changed save our mode of thinking, and thus we drift towards unparalleled disaster.*' Albert Einstein.

What exactly is problematic about our models of thinking? When we look deeply into our thinking for the past 4,000 years we see one all-pervasive form. We see images of pyramids, of ladders and of vertical power relations frozen in time. We see hierarchies, the structures of fear and ego, dominator, 'power over others' models of relating.

Humanity is in crisis. There is an urgent need for a deep change in human consciousness. The old hierarchical and capitalistic ways of thinking and relating have not solved the world's problems. But what can we put in their place? A half-hearted belief that equality is a rather good thing is simply not enough. I want to suggest that we need a new consciousness in which equalizing is the very essence of our belief system, not just an optional extra. Equalizing is a primal creative force and can even be called the spirit in matter.

But with the new belief, we need new structures in our psyches. Today, they are still largely organized by internal power hierarchies, based on fear. Psychological change towards internal balancing can give us the freedom to live more in tune with the energies and rhythms around us, to act appropriately and increase equality. With equality comes the ability to empathize that is so often lacking in the world today. An equalizing philosophy can be healthier for people, as well as more useful for sustaining the planet than the prevailing hierarchical model.

In a hierarchy the opposites are divided vertically with one always dominating the other. One has to win. One is seen as rigidly superior to the other. Using this paradigm, thinking must control feeling, and humans must control nature. But there are millions of more subtle hierarchies too. This vertical way of thinking actually underlies many of our psychological problems. Low self-esteem comes from feeling lower than others. Looking down on others stops us empathizing with them. Many personal relationships start flowing rhythmically and then quickly deteriorate into power struggles. Unlearning these old paradigms and replacing them with equalizing rhythmic models could help us personally as well as socially in many ways.

Most of us start life within frameworks of hundreds of vertically divided, unbalanced opposites. I have many examples from my psychotherapy practice. Let's call this client Ian. He grew up as a sensitive only child in a small mining town. His working class mother had a strong desire to better the family and go up in the world. She pushed her bright son to work hard, and he eventually gained a place at a good college. However in his unconscious there was a deep sense of shame coming from the class hierarchy in his head.

Ian was driven to pursue beautiful rich women. This created yet another vertical model in his mind, in which the women embodied the perfection that he lacked. He felt even more inferior as the ugly, imperfect one. After a particularly painful rejection he joined a left wing party. Soon everything made sense. The class hierarchy of labor and capital underlay all the other inequalities of life. He became more and more angry, went on many demonstrations, helped to edit the party's paper and saw history in Marxist terms.

Ian then became a history teacher in a poor inner city community, and continued with his political life. He rarely went home. Secretly he despised his own working class father. But he had begun to idealize the local party leader. He accepted the vertical thinking within the party and believed every word the leader spoke. Four years later he married a sensible middle class women, who ran a nice well-organized home and two children for him. Ian had arrived, somewhere. But the shame lived on unconsciously and combined with the kind low self-esteem that no material success could change.

In his thirties Ian found Buddhism, which gave him some peace for a while. But he had simply replaced the political leader with a male spiritual teacher to look up to. This Buddhist organization also turned out to be quite hierarchical. After a few years of meditating he began to increase his self-esteem by feeling superior to others who had not been doing it for so long. Then he started therapy and began to change his mental models. His self-esteem was genuinely increased, but at the same time he lowered his omnipotent dreams of needing to be perfect and save the world. He began to learn to flow with the rhythm of life as it happens rather than trying to control it out of fear he would be 'found out' as an inferior being. Instead of wildly swinging moods of extreme confidence and depression he accepted the vulnerable side and his considerable strengths. He started visiting his parents more often, and campaigned against injustice, but in a less angry way.

Equalizing Rhythmic Attunement

Equalizing Rhythmic Attunement can be called ERA for short. Era also happens to be the name of an ancient Greek goddess, the female counterpart to Eros who is described in myth as being the first to set in motion the rhythm of life out of chaos. She represents the equalizing spirit in matter that ancient and native peoples understood so well. It is likely that the early goddesses and their companions, the serpents, were symbolic representations of the primal spirit in matter and only became specific personalities later. Barbara Walker[14] writes that another version of Era was Rhea, which actually means 'the flow'. Both were forms of the

Great Goddess of early Aegean civilization (8000 – 2000 BC) who predated the appearance of God on the scene around 2000 – 4000 BC.

It seems that ancient agricultural peoples of the world kept alive the knowing of the equalizing spirit in matter through a spirituality that centred on the rhythms of nature. Archaeologists like James Mellart [15] noticed that they were egalitarian societies with equal sized homes and graves. And curiously they all seemed to have similar spiritual symbols. From Africa to Ireland, Bulgaria to Crete, there were found images of snakes and spirals carved in stone, painted on temple walls or pots. The archaeo-mythologist Marija Gimbutas[16] argues that these same symbols that she found all over the region she calls Old Europe, show an awareness of the mysterious flow of life.

Lucy Goodison [17] describes how in ancient Crete around 2000 BC there were many images showing an understanding of the interconnect-edness of opposites in nature and humans. Later this changed and the art became less fluid and more suggestive of the change over to hierarchical thinking. Riane Eisler [18], Anne Baring and Jules Cashford [19], all write about the dramatic change that brought in patriarchal, war-like, dominator cultures to the settled peoples of Asia, Africa and Europe whose spirituality was based on flow.

Is there a link between a culture's spirituality and art based on flow and the interconnection of opposites, and peaceful, egalitarian lifestyles? Many scholars such as Erich Fromm [20] in the *Anatomy of Human Destructiveness* think there was. In Chatal Huyuk 5000 BC, the houses and burials were largely the same size. As there was no writing we cannot know for sure exactly what they believed, but the images on their walls showed a sophisticated understanding of the opposites of life and death, creation and destruction, masculine and feminine. Significantly there was not a single image of warfare.

In his important book *The Fall* Steve Taylor [21] argues that a massive change happened in the world between around 4000 BC and 2000 BC away from egalitarian societies towards hierarchical ones. Some people think that it was the move to settled towns itself that created the change, but he points out that there were at least 4,000 years of peaceful settlement from around 8000 BC before the change happened.

He shows that the transition to patriarchy and hierarchy started when climate change turned large, highly populated areas in Africa, Asia and Europe into deserts. This apparently turned peaceful peoples into competitive, war loving tribes with hierarchical religions and societies. But then, after what he calls The Fall, religion and culture kept the hierarchical paradigm going, to influence most of the rest of the world by around 4000 BC and up to this very day.

Minoan Crete from 3000 BC – 1,400 BC seems to have been the last of the 'old' societies to keep the rhythmic paradigm central to its culture. It was known even in ancient Egypt for its advanced spiritual development, probably due to its sophisticated ability to attune to the energies and rhythms of nature. Although we cannot go back, we can look at what

made those more equal societies work for so long. Are there clues in the life loving rhythms of their spiritual and cultural life? As Platon [22] described, ancient Cretan art shows how the people showed 'delight in beauty, grace and movement'. Even the poet Sappho [23] writes in the Classical Greek period, wistfully, of the joy of girls dancing in ancient Crete, a thousand years earlier.. 'In the young spring evening, The moon is shining full, girls form a circle, as though round

Cretan Love

an altar. And their feet perform, Rhythmical steps, Like the soft feet of Cretan girls, must once have danced.'

Natural Ethics

Today many of us are beginning to try and unlearn hierarchical thinking and relearn the sense of deep equality that seems to have come so naturally to us in ancient times. Modern humans were already developed physically, exactly as we are now, at least 150,000 years ago. For most of that time we lived in tune with nature using spirituality to help us. We did not feel superior to her, as we do now .It was our later cultures, our myths of heroic conquest, our vertical thinking and organizing that changed us.

We learnt very young, to fit in with those new hierarchic cultures, largely through fear. But we had to learn; the paradigm was not inborn, and now we are changing again. Both the rhythm models and the hierarchic ones are constructs, created and learnt by humans. There is no evidence that these are genetically determined models of thought. They may be deeply ingrained, and hard to change, but that is very different from saying that they are innate. The debate on the question of what is nature and what is nurture continues, and probably always will. Meanwhile, we can only try to work with the extraordinary capacity of humans to change and adapt

With all the old stories being questioned, many of us no longer look to God/Goddess or even to pure reason or utilitarianism to guide us in our lives. Can this idea of attunement to rhythms be used as a practical philosophy for living? Instead of struggling to attain perfection or enlightenment, can we focus on learning to attune to the equalizing rhythms inside and outside us? The aim becomes attunement rather than happiness or status. Aiming only for individual happiness usually results in deep dissatisfaction. And desperation for status is part of our underlying hierarchical mind set, and the cause of even more dissatisfaction and unhappiness. Whatever we achieve never feels quite enough.

There are many hopeful signs that this equalizing rhythmic model is already being implicitly used in many areas of social transformation at the beginning of the 21st Century, from progressive politics to the rave culture. But it is usually in conflict with the old hierarchical paradigm. Modern life can seem like a struggle between the two paradigms. One recent example is the backlash against feminism. Another is the use of terms like 'politically correct' to denigrate concerns about all kinds of inequalities, from race to poverty.

The Inner Rebel

Fortunately for the human race, there seems to be a healthy inner rebel inside us that is especially tuned in to inequalities and imbalances. We explore this more later. But it is important to make a distinction between the neurotic inner rebel who is unconsciously turning everyone in authority into parental figures that they are angry with, and the wise inner rebel that needs to be honored and worked with. Ways of doing this are described throughout the book. This whole project could be seen as a training in rebelling at the deepest levels, by refusing to obey the voices of the hierarchies we have internalized. By remembering to listen to our wise inner rebel every day, we can realize how trapped we are in the vertical paradigm. We begin to see the powerful mind prisons that squeeze our naturally flowing energies into rigid patterns of ups and downs, winning and losing and all the hierarchies that rule us.

Most of the post modernists like Michael Foucault[24] who have analyzed the internalized vertical power structures everywhere in society, seem to see them as inevitable. Those at the bottom collude by finding mutual support in the hierarchies. The psychoanalyst Lacan[25] saw them so embedded in the language we learn from earliest childhood, that we can never escape. Opposites may indeed be present in most languages but do they have to be hierarchically arranged with one always above the other? Perhaps we can consciously learn to do different things with the opposites and turn them from being vertical to being horizontal and ever-changing.

So many of the metaphors we use in everyday life come from this vertical mind-set. We talk of targets to be reached, problems to be attacked, good to win out over evil. As Bush famously said before the invasion of Iraq, 'You are either with us or against us.' Millions of people all over the world reacted not only to the actual war, but to the hierarchical thinking behind it.

In spite of the increasing use of the new equalizing paradigm, the old vertical structures are still powerful. For example, there are millions of spiritual searchers who, on the one hand, are learning to tune in to the rhythmic flow of life, but still create unbalanced organizations with gurus at the top. Millions of people campaigning for justice and equality create rigid, hierarchical, revolutionary political parties. There may always be some hierarchies, and in a few areas they may even be getting stronger. But there is also an important trend today that is moving away from them. This book explores that trend and suggests equalizing rhythms as an alternative structure to the rigid verticals of the past.

Things to do: Exploring the Opposites

1. Remember a time when you were living in the flow. What was different? What happened? How did it feel? What do you think were the factors that made this state possible? What factors help you personally to be more in the flow?

2. Write your life story in terms of the hierarchies and vertical opposites that framed your life. Describe times when you were at the bottom of a hierarchy, and times when you were at the top. How did it feel?

3. Write about the times when the vertical opposites were transformed in some way.

CHAPTER TWO

TURNING LADDERS INTO SNAKES

Many people in the West are becoming less deferential to authority figures. When we go to the doctor today we are likely to be armed with sheets of information about our problem, downloaded from the internet. Children no longer expect parents or teachers to always know best. Most of us are less impressed than our parents were by people who are upper class, or of high rank in the organizations we work for and we are less likely to put up with being disrespected ourselves by those authority figures or higher ranking individuals.

This transformation could be described as a subtle equalizing process, happening at all levels of society all over the world in different ways. Robert Fuller[1] writing in the US calls it a 'dignitarian' movement, as vital today as the feminist one was in the 1970s. He describes the problem as 'rankism' and argues for the dissolving of strict and unnecessary hierarchies in offices and institutions. His book has been a recent best seller in the US. Millions seem to be tuning into the idea of questioning unnecessary hierarchy in organizations.

However in non-Western cultures, the most important hierarchy affecting people's lives may not be within organizations, but between dominating Western cultural hegemony and local ways of life. For example, for many Muslim girls, wearing the hijab is a mark of resistance to Western superiority. In their lives it may be even more important than the power of gender hierarchies.

Every group, every culture and every age seems to have its own hierarchical problems and its own forms of resistance. But underneath them all is the deeply ingrained structure of superior and inferior. It is the coat hanger on which everything is hung.

The everyday use of the word 'hierarchy' is not usually related to thought structures. It is most often applied to social structures in which the superior group rules over the inferior one, who may then in turn rule over another group inferior to them. Inclusion of the term '-archy' means 'ruling'. Monarchy is a hierarchical social structure in which kings or queens rule their subjects. The basic vertical image has lain deep in our human thinking for thousands of years. It is time to change it.

The Philosophy of Equality

The word 'equality' has been given so many different meanings, and has even sometimes become quite meaningless. It has been used and misused as a slogan for almost all modern politicians, including those talking about 'equal development' in Apartheid South Africa. In this book I try to reclaim it as a primal process, as the spirit in matter, as a psychology and a philosophy.

In the theory of ERA, all levels of reality have in common a kind of endless rhythmic equalization and this is mirrored in our ideas of a natural human justice underneath all the laws constructed by societies. JJ Bachofen[2] called it the Ius Naturale (natural law) that existed in Europe before the Romans. He described it as law of the mother who loves all her children equally. It belonged to earlier pre-patriarchal, pre-hierarchical times.

By including the word 'equalizing' a human value is being brought into a neutral natural phenomenon. The use of the word 'equalize' suggests connections between natural processes and human justice. The connection is through the underlying rhythmic forms or shapes of the processes. On political and social levels we are forever shifting the balances of power. The resistance to imbalances and injustices has continued through history, reflecting the rhythmic natural processes.

Progressive and creative people are generally against hierarchies. And everyone talks about equality as a good thing. But all too often it is seen more like a static goal to be attained one day in Utopia, than a process. It can imply sameness, as in 'equality feminism' which Germaine Greer[3] describes with contempt. She thinks of it as women striving to become like men. Or it is seen as limited to equal rights, equal pay or equal value, important though these are. But here it is suggested that the equalization processes goes on in complex interrelated ways at all levels of personal, social and environmental life.

Equalizing rhythm can be seen as the opposite of hierarchy. It is flexible while hierarchy is rigid. It flows from tops to bottoms and back again. There is no permanent top or bottom. In the new holistic worldview, rhythm may be the new mental model. Without it, new ideas, even holistic ones, can easily get squeezed back into the old hierarchical forms. The word 'holistic' suggests interconnectedness, but through what forms are the separate elements connected? Are they connected hierarchically, merged into one big thing, or do they stay different but dance together, connected through balancing forces?

These rhythmic processes occur on so many interrelated levels at once, but the basic form is the same whatever scale or level we are analyzing. When one side or extreme is reached there is a move back to its opposite. The concept of 'equalizing rhythmic processes' is simply a new way of describing the endless balancing forces of the universe, familiar to ecologists and psychologists, Taoists and mystics, philosophers and healers, past and present.

Dance of the Opposites

Every day we all act and think with the old hierarchical paradigm and with the new rhythmic one. They are sometimes almost simultaneous, sometimes in conflict, and often unconscious. When we put a celebrity on a pedestal or look down on someone who is different, we are in the old way of thinking. When we look them in the eye as equal human beings with respect, we are using the new paradigm. When our minds are always busy planning future goals, we are in the old way. When we consciously tune in to our breathing rhythms in the present, we are in the new rhythm.

Rhythms and Hierarchies in the Global Picture

These two paradigms are also played out on a global scale. It may seem on the surface as though the world stage is all about one hierarchy competing with or dominating another. At the same time the very idea of vertical organization and thinking is being questioned. There are millions of people all over the world thinking differently. Even the new anti global capitalist ways of organizing against injustices are relatively non-hierarchical. There are no leaders, just spokespeople and networks and instant information through the internet. Similarly, concepts of sustainability are all about ecological balance, not endless economic growth, which is a vertical, goal-orientated idea. One directional growth with no reversal in the opposite direction would be a disaster in nature. Imagine trying to breath in forever, without allowing the out breath! Yet this model is deeply implanted in our heads. The idea of hierarchical growth still runs our economies and helps create world suffering.

The deepest conflict today is not just between the traditional and the modern, in which the modern seems to be winning. It's not primarily a clash between civilizations in which the West is expecting to win. It may not even be purely a struggle between capitalism and socialism in which capitalism is believed to have already won. It is not only between the ruling and the working classes, developing and developed worlds – although massive hierarchies of difference dominate our planet with obscene inequalities increasing worldwide. Hidden underneath all the conflicts and transformations in the world today is a primal tension between all vertical ways of thinking and structures and the alternative paradigm of rhythmic, equalizing and balancing processes.

This tension has probably always existed, but especially since the 'fall' around 6,000 years ago. However, it seems to be taking particular and intense forms today. Hierarchy at one level may create more of it at another level. Anger at the superior attitude of the West plays a part in the rise of Islamic fundamentalism. This seems to strengthen its own internal hierarchies. The progressive journalist Richard Goldstein [4] argues that the rise of all religious fundamentalisms is directly related to the feminist demand for sexual equality. If we think on a long-term

Pyramids of Thinking in a Sea of Rhythm

scale, the recent shift to gender equality is massive after at least 5,000 years of patriarchy. It is scary for men. And there has been a deep but subtle backlash. But now we need to talk of the end of all hierarchies, not just gender ones. The 20th Century was full of attempts to change them, from the civil rights movement to anti-colonialism, from class struggle to votes for women. Yet it is extraordinary how deeply the vertical paradigm of hierarchy is still embedded within us all. Is it inevitable, genetic, universal? Are we psychologically programmed to think in terms of superior and inferior forever? If not how can we change?

Rhythms and Hierarchies in the Personal Picture

Many psychologists have argued in the past that hierarchical thinking is a learnt paradigm, passed on through culture via the family and schools early in our lives. William Reich [5], Erich Fromm [6], and others have described in detail this learnt internalization of vertical social structures. It creates the authoritarian personality and a fear of freedom. But today other psychologists and therapists such as the fashionable Adam Phillips[6] seem to accept it as inevitable. 'Without this superiority existing somewhere in a person's orbit, they – we – are destitute.' What a depressing statement. This comes from his book titled *Equals.* [7]

It is clear that our inner worlds are interrelated in complex ways with the outer ones of society, economics and politics. Each situation and context brings its own sets of hierarchies and imbalances. But under much of the complexity is still the basic model of dividing things and people into inferior and superior. As well as material disadvantages resulting from massive external inequality, there can be subtle psychological impacts too. Internalized social hierarchies can create depression through feelings of inferiority and powerlessness as well as through external economic problems. Franz Fanon[8] wrote about this in connection with racial hierarchies. He noticed how many black people learnt to think of themselves as lesser than whites, and may even try to act white to compensate for those feelings.

I had a client we will call Amina who is 24 years old. Her parents came from Pakistan in the 1960s. They ran a shop and suffered from the deep but casual racism of everyday life in a Western city. Amina's father was an avid reader of English literature and wrote poetry. He was very encouraging to her and pushed her to go to university and become a writer herself. Neither of her parents were religious and they wanted to align themselves with mainstream modern society. While at university Amina met and began living with a white fellow student. Her parents were deeply conflicted about this despite their modernism, but tried to understand. Amina herself had largely rejected her own roots and hid any inferiority feelings very well. She was a very confident young woman on the surface.

Yet after leaving university she gave up her dreams of being a writer and took a job as a youth worker instead. It was while she was working there that she met many radicalized young Muslims and began to wonder about her own background. She became depressed and came to therapy at this point. At first she was skeptical about the world of therapy, let alone religion, believing only in science. She did not trust intuition, deep feeling or indeed anything to do with the spiritual. Then she started having vivid dreams. One was about an abandoned house that psychotherapeutically represented her own feeling of emptiness inside.

Much of the work was about deeply internalized unconscious racism and sexism. At first she talked contemptuously about the 'backward' Muslim girls wearing the hijab and the family members holding on to the 'old' ways. It was clear that she only valued masculine ways of thinking. She even despised her own body. Gradually she began to fill that 'empty house' with pride in her background and in her 'feminine' side. She also started to trust her intuition more as she kept meeting relatives when on the tube or waiting at bus stops miles away from where they lived. She recognized that there seemed to be a message about her family and cultural background.

At this time by chance her boyfriend discovered Sufism which is the more mystical aspect of Islam. At first Amina was horrified. But eventually she became interested herself and discovered all the beauty and wisdom from her own tradition. The old hierarchies of modern and 'backward', science and spirituality, masculine and feminine began to dissolve. She was more able to flow between them all and stop looking down on people that she was projecting her own inferiorities on to.

Unconscious hierarchical thinking can even cause the repression of unacceptable sides of ourselves, such as our angry or vulnerable aspects, which are seen as 'lower'. Then we project those unacceptable sides onto other individuals and groups believed to be 'lesser'. So we have the belief that say, all black people are angry or all women are soft, when really we just can't accept the angry or soft sides of ourselves. In fact our socially constructed hierarchies, involving negative comparisons with others cause many of our individual and collective neuroses as Oliver James[9] has shown in *Affluenza*.

The equalizing paradigm associated with rhythm and flow helps us accept all sides of ourselves and others. It underlies the ability to hold ambiguity and paradox, rather than splitting everything into vertical opposites. It enables us to trust the rhythmic wisdom of our own deepest intuition rather than listening to authorities or conventions.

Jane is a green activist and very pro-equality in relation to politics, but psychologically she was struggling with her deep internalized hierarchies. She came in to therapy at the age of 29, stressed out and depressed. She grew up in a middle class family, as the oldest daughter of an alcoholic mother. Jane had to be responsible from a very young age, but now she feels responsible for the whole world. There is some guilt about her privileged upbringing. As this was explored early in our work together, she began to see that it was not so wonderful at home.

Jane talks angrily about the massive global inequalities of north and south, humans and animals and the arms trade leading to the greatest inequality of all, taking another's life. She is active in the movement against the arms trade. But in the squat where she lives there is inequality. Jane worships her boyfriend and feels lower than him because she thinks he is more attractive and intelligent than she is. She does most of the cooking and cleaning for everyone. She always puts others first and was afraid not to be in control. Coming to see a therapist was the first time she had done something just for herself. At first much of our work was to encourage her to be more in touch with her own everyday rhythmic needs. She started to rest more, not go out on every single protest, and do less housework.

With this new-found balance in her outer life, she was able to start looking at her inner hierarchies. As Jane valued herself more she stopped looking up to her boyfriend so much. She got angry about her mother as well as injustices in the world. Jane could never trust her mother to look after her. In fact any kind of trust was hard and she had always been very anti-religion, so there was no traditional God to rely on. But her deep love of nature led her towards goddess spirituality and a faith in the power of mother earth herself. She began to trust her own intuition and found herself more and more living in the flow. Jane developed an inner freedom that did not turn her into a totally individualist hedonist or stop her being an activist. She was in many ways more effective, finding herself nearly always in the right place at the right time.

Rhythm as the Dynamic of Psychological Freedom

Instead of thinking of ourselves as solid permanent beings, we can describe ourselves as continuously equalizing rhythmic processes. As Erich Fromm[10] showed, it is out of a fear of freedom that we develop rigid identities and big egos. We call ourselves a doctor or a journalist, Christian or Muslim, a Londoner or a New Yorker, belonging to one sub culture or another. Being nothing but lots of interconnected flowing processes sounds too diffuse – we may lose our sense of identity. But maybe it is only when we are free psychologically as well as physically that we can truly 'go with flow'.

Then we can be both strong and vulnerable, sad and joyful at different times. But we are not totally identified with either of the opposite states. What we are is the flow itself, the movement between them, beings who can never be entirely captured in any still and static category. I am suggesting that to be fully human, healthy and alive is to have equalizing rhythmic processes constantly balancing in and around us.

Unfortunately, internal as well as external hierarchical structures distort these processes. They can do it directly, as when we feel depressed because we are being put down at work, at home or in society in general. But this lowering of our position in life leads to other ways of stopping us being in the flow. For example, we may then eat too much, to comfort ourselves. This puts our body's natural balancing mechanisms out of synch. Or indirectly, we can have ideas of success and failure which depress us when our lives don't match the ideas of perfection we have set up for ourselves.

Freedom is a complex concept. I am using it in the sense of being empty enough of mental baggage to be fully attuned to equalizing rhythmic processes in the moment. Fortunately, these processes do tend to go on without our help. Our dreams are often desperately trying to compensate, balance up our daytime inequalities. Our bodies are even more determinedly trying to keep us balanced, despite what rubbish we put into them, or what rigid ideas we try and control them with.

Unconscious rhythmic processes seem to go on throughout nature. What may be unique about homo sapiens is that we have the capacity to attune consciously to these rhythms. We can listen out for signs of imbalance with our intuitive minds.

Attuning to Our Deepest Intuition

The word 'intuition' has many meanings. One way of describing freedom is being able to obey no authority other than your deepest intuition. It is being able to live in the present, attuning action, thought and feeling to the equalizing rhythms present in that moment. In one situation this might mean rebelling against the authority, say of the state imposing unjust laws. In another situation it might mean acting with authority, for example commanding a child not to cross a busy road. Can we develop the freedom to be appropriate?

It probably takes a lifetime to get to know oneself well enough to work out what is deepest intuition, and what comes from neuroses. Freedom is also about bringing up all those lower repressed sides of ourselves, so they no longer rule us. When we admit, face, acknowledge these unacceptable feelings they have less power over us. Apart from the fact that we are less likely to act on them in some way, acceptance helps to empty us of all that associated guilt and anxiety. When these feelings fill us up, our minds are too full and noisy for us to be able to listen to our deepest intuition. Full minds are not free.

It is very freeing to accept all sides of ourselves equally. In fact you could say that freedom is also about accepting the self and the other, and life exactly as it is, without preferring it to be different. How things are and how they should be is a vertical model with all the shoulds in a superior position. Accepting what *is* does not stop us acting to redress injustices and imbalances in the world. These involve equalizing rhythmic processes of a different order. Acceptance can be seen as one kind of psychological freedom.

The rational mind can play a part in consciously attuning us to many different equa-rhythmic processes. For example, it could be used in working out ways of reducing the appalling inequalities in the world. But knowing that such inequalities are wrong tends to come from the deepest intuition. Reason can argue anything, one way or the other. It is clever but not wise. Reason can tell us many ways of reducing inequality in the world from ending the arms trade to increasing redistribution from rich to poor countries. But if there is not the basic deep attunement to equalizing, a spirituality with equality at its core, such changes are unlikely to happen.

Freedom can also be an ability to hold, or dance between, the apparent contradictory opposites of full equal acceptance of what is, and the passion for acting to equalize where there is inequality.

So exactly how can we use this model to become more free?

These are three approaches to transformations through equalizing rhythms:

1. Conscious attunement. A cognitive psychology approach in which we work out   what our main internal and interpersonal opposites and hierarchies are. Then we find out which opposites needs to be strengthened in order to equalize. We also learn more rhythmic ways of thinking about life.

2. Unconscious attunement. We learn techniques of stilling the mind and emptying it of overwhelming thoughts/feelings, so that we can be more open to the unconscious rhythmic processes of our intuitive wisdom in the present.

3. Rhythmic attunement between the conscious and unconscious. We bring the suppressed unconscious into consciousness and we affect the unconscious through conscious imagination.

Things to do: Exploring Freedom through Balancing Inner Opposites
1. Think of an area of your life where you do not feel free. It might be that you feel stuck in a relationship or job. Maybe you are too touchy when people put you down. Or like many people you find social gatherings stressful. Perhaps you are too scared of authority to stick up against injustice in ways you know intuitively are right.

Then think of the main opposites involved. For example, it could be that for you dependence and independence are major opposites. Perhaps you have swung from one to the other unconsciously, as when adolescents separate totally from parents and can then become symbiotically dependent on a girlfriend or wife. Later the same person can swing to longing for complete independence. End of relationship!

Instead think about the opposites as both needed, but at different times. Work out which of the opposites is stronger right now. Then decide how the other side can be increased. If you are too dependent at present, find more independent things to do.

These opposites might relate to others. For example, there is the desire for closeness and the fear of intimacy. And underneath these could be the opposites of expansion (love) and contraction (fear). How can both opposites be danced with, responding appropriately to circumstances. Sometimes it is necessary to contract, protect, withdraw and at other times it is appropriate to open, take risks, and love.

2. In this un-free situation what are the main hierarchies that you have learnt? For example in a scary social situation like a party where you don't know anyone, you might feel inferior in some way. Are people who

know each other superior to strangers? Is there a sense that they are all clever and you are stupid? Or are they all pretty or good looking and you are not? Or is it the other way round and you meet someone you automatically look down on. Are they wearing the wrong trainers or are they simply too old or working class to be worth your attention? When you get home write down all the hierarchies present in your head. Check them out.

3. Practice equalizing by visualizing one of the people that you either looked up to or looked down on and imagine them as totally equal to you. Look them straight in the eye and say to yourself I am equal to you and you are equal to me. Practice with friends or lovers if they let you.

4. Take a large sheet of paper and draw a line down the middle. Then think about all the main opposites in your life and write them on either side of your line. Then decide which pairs are fairly balanced in a rhythmic relation to each other, and which ones are lopsided. What do you need to do in your life to equalize the imbalanced ones?

It could include opposites like too much work and not enough play, or like pleasing others too much and needing to be more 'selfish'. Everyone has their own most appropriate personal rhythms. Even on a physical level, some of us are night people and other are early morning people.

5. Next time you are about to enter an un-free zone, spend half an hour emptying your mind of all hierarchies, assumptions and even thoughts of any kind if you can. It helps to count your breathing, so your mind is busy and your focus is on the rhythm of breath, instead of being full of hierarchical thoughts. Try to keep remembering to come back to the equalizing rhythms of the breath whenever you can. The breath is a powerful ongoing reminder of the way one opposite (out) naturally flows back into the other (in).

6. Write down your dreams for a week. Applying the model of unconscious equalizing, see if you can work out what unbalanced aspect of your waking life the dreams might be trying to compensate.

7. Take a large sheet of paper and think of two opposites inside you

like good little girl and wild woman, or bossy and timid sides. Draw a line down the middle and paint two pictures to represent the two aspects of you. Notice the differences and which one you prefer. Explore and try identifying with the one you least prefer. With other people you could have a go at acting them both out. And finally set up a dialogue between them and see what they have to say to each other.

CHAPTER THREE

LOVING REBELLION

During the French Revolution, on November 10th 1793, in Paris, a most
unusual ceremony was held in the Cathedral of Notre Dame. Instead of
the worship of Jesus and the Virgin Mary, it was held to celebrate Liberty,
Equality and Reason. According to historians[1] describing the event, the
ideals of the revolution were embodied by a woman wearing a blue cloak
with oak leaves on her head. She rode on the shoulders of four young men
and girls crowned with oak leaves were her attendants. This temporary
'goddess' was installed in a temple built specially on a mound actually
inside the Cathedral. Hundreds of ordinary citizens filled the ornate space
with songs of the revolution. It must have been an extraordinary scene
that day, at the very center of the old patriarchal religious power in Paris.

In the early years of the revolution there seems to have been a serious
attempt to create a kind of secular spirituality, honoring the human need
for a sense of the sacred and a deep connectedness to nature. Indeed it was
not only in Paris that such creative connections were being made. It is a
little known fact that during this time churches all over France were
turned into Temples of Reason and Philosophy. Trees of Liberty were
ceremoniously planted everywhere. It could have been the beginning of a
whole new culture uniting revolutionary ideas and a natural, secular spirituality. But sadly it was short lived.

Since then there has been at best, an uneasy relationship between
progressive politics and spirituality, and at worst, downright antagonism.
Religion as 'the opium of the people' has been the battle cry of the Left,
while the quieter belief of Engels in dialectics 'as the spirit in matter' was
forgotten. The distinction between 'religions' as organized, hierarchical
systems and 'spiritualities' as attuning to natural energies has generally
been overlooked. However if we extend spirituality, to include the energy

of love and compassion for the oppressed, it has always flowed in the veins of revolutionaries. As Che Guevara once famously said, 'At the risk of sounding ridiculous, let me say that a revolutionary is guided by great feelings of love.' Yet this core motivation has too often been forgotten. Instead most revolutionaries and left wing activists identify themselves as hard and purely rational warriors fighting against an enemy 'other'. The hierarchical paradigm of win or lose – down with X, destroy Y, attack Z – can still be heard on the streets at most mass demonstrations. It is simplistically dualistic, with no room for the complexities of the many different inequalities or for attunement to the rhythms of the flow. Many people who believe in equality and justice are deeply unhappy individuals not living at all rhythmically in their daily lives.

A client we will call Sarah grew up with Marxist parents and spent her childhood delivering political leaflets around their neighborhood. She was naturally active on the Left at University. But after her first important relationship ended, Sarah became depressed. She felt empty and lonely in spite of having so many friends. She began having some extraordinary dreams in which she was visited by a golden angelic presence and experienced a deep sense of peace. The feeling was the complete opposite of what she felt in everyday life. Secretly Sarah began to read about spirituality. She went to a Buddhist meditation class, hoping to find calm and contentment. But sitting in silence only made her mind race all the faster at first.

There was so much shame around this longing for the peace she had experienced in the dream that Sarah could not tell anyone. Her family and friends were fiercely anti-religion. It was years before she came to therapy and began meditating seriously. Talking about her experiences was a relief in itself, and realizing that it did not have to be in conflict with her political beliefs, helped too. She even began to see that looking down on other people's spiritual experiences from a superior left wing intellectual stance was itself oppressive. She later returned to university to study anthropology and studied the spiritual practices of Native

Americans with far more respect than she would have been capable of while still in a place of intellectual contempt.

Sarah's story is not uncommon. There is an increasing interest in religious matters amongst progressives, if only because of the influence of radical Islam, seeing Muslims as the new oppressed group. For others there is also a personal longing for something as well as reason, some more meaningful connection to the bigger world, even some kind of spirituality. The time may have come for progressive politics to develop a new spiritual core. Some deep passion, some juice from the loins, some heart felt conviction, all too often seems to be missing today. Our 'rage for equality' got lost while furnishing our houses.

In the West at least, there has been a mood of despair. Alongside the rise and rise of consumerist global capitalism, left wing ideologies have been battered for decades. The academic, post-modern contempt for all 'grand narratives' has given them the death blow from within. And the accusatory use of the term 'political correctness' has all but finished them off on the mainstream streets. We live in a cool, ironic age, scornful of almost any passion for anything, especially ideas. Yet even progressives now talk politely about 'values' not beliefs, single issues rather than whole visions, rearranging the deck chairs on the Titanic as it sinks. More and more people who were once idealistic are becoming depressed.

Many individuals, even some progressives, are arguing that we have already got 'too much equality' in the West. They think multiculturalism has failed and feminism has gone too far. But instead of replying with piecemeal arguments about particular situations, the problems could be defined as not nearly enough equality in general, in all aspects of life. It can seem as though we are still in the Stone Age as far as equalizing our societies, locally and globally. We have been using crude hammers, like state communism, rather than sophisticated tools to fashion something as beautiful as deep equality. How different it would be if there was a widespread, passionate belief in equality as a guiding force on all levels of life. Imagine a new progressive spirituality with equalizing at its heart,

evolving slowly but surely in the hidden corners of the collective unconscious, on the peninsular outposts of mainland thinking, on the streets and
of course on line too. Although this may seem like an impossible dream,
it is actually already happening. Underneath the general widespread
materialism and hierarchical party politics this new approach is quietly
being born.

Natural Spirituality and Protest

A client called Samantha came to therapy at the age of 28 deeply
depressed at the state of the world. She had been a full time Green activist
and was now completely burnt out. She had also recently started a
relationship with an older journalist. He was a kind of father figure.
Samantha described him as brilliant and knowledgeable, well read and in
fact, almost perfect. Through his influence she too became cynical about
human nature and the possibilities of change. It seemed to them both that
the whole human race was doomed. What was the point of taking action?
In the end it was this sense of hopelessness that drove her into depression.
In therapy we worked on her low self-esteem especially around her
perceived lack of intellectual abilities. She began to stand up to her
boyfriend, disagree and even get angry with him.

She also began to experience herself as more deeply interconnected
with others and nature. This meant that every little action and thought
matters. In our later sessions we would sometimes sit in silence honoring
the equality and presence of these two humans in the room. Then we
would sit and honor our equality with the plants in the room and be
present with them. We noticed and laughed whenever an unhelpful hierarchical or controlling thought popped into either of our heads. We were
fully present and in the flow. Samantha tuned in more to her personal
rhythms of rest and activity, sleeping for ten hours a night for months.
Her political activities became more part-time, and very importantly her
hopefulness returned.

There needs to be hope. Hope in itself is radical. Without it, millions simply accept the status quo and feel powerless. The hopeful signs of the new paradigm are there. They can be seen during protests, in social centers squatted by young anarchists, at festivals, conferences and alternative raves. And the essence of both the new political and the new spiritual is that they are determinedly non-hierarchical. Instead of the vertical, pyramid shape to everything in conventional politics and religion, the shapes are circular, spiraling, rhythmic. A new way of thinking is developing alongside the activism. Of course it's not entirely new to feminists, alternative socialists and anarchists of the past. But a greater openness to the spiritual dimensions is very different.

This spirituality is far from the Methodist chapels of the old British Labor movement or even the religion based inter-faith initiatives of progressive Rabbis and Priests – although all these have their value. But now there is also a grass roots movement tuned into the rhythms of nature. It works with energies, not just slogans. It has influences from Paganism, Buddhism, Hinduism, Sufism, as well as many other spiritualities, but it does not adhere to any of these as organized hierarchical religions. It is more about finding a common natural spirituality and exploring the question as to what it means to be human.

One of the main inspirers of this movement is Starhawk[2], an activist from California. Since the late 1970s she has been advocating and practicing what she sometimes calls goddess spirituality and sometimes calls witchcraft or magic in combination with protesting against injustice. She has always been aware of the difficulties some politically orientated feminists have with the 'goddess'. But she argues that it is an active spirituality, because 'goddess' is immanent in nature not some supernatural authority to obey. The goal is harmony with nature, and following that goal involves being able to tune into the balancing flow in whatever context one finds oneself. It could be about stopping the cutting down of trees or demonstrating against the arms trade. The question is always, Where is the flow guiding me?

Going with the flow in some contexts can be a life and death matter, a revolutionary act of transgression, not just a 'fluffy' way of life. But to live with that guidance it is vital to have inner clarity. This requires listening to our deepest intuition and not being too clouded with hatred or fear. Working through these valid but often overwhelming feelings is an important part of the process.

A lot of 'psychotherapy' happens informally during these events. I once ran a workshop for anti-road building activists to help them explore and safely express their anger. The aim was to free them up from personal 'stuff' to then be able to act on the protest according to the flow and needs of the moment.

At times it may include transforming negative energies into positive ones. An Israeli friend did a ritual on an anti war march using the word Esh used by soldiers to fire guns. She turned it into the power of fire energy to transform hatred into love by forming a ritual circle, chanting and dancing. Sometimes it requires standing up to authority, using warrior energy. At other times activists need to sit down in a circle and be strong and still. But it always demands attunement first. Listening to our deepest intuition enables us to trust the flow of natural energies on the side of justice. These energy flows may be given names of goddesses like Rhea or Themis. A formal ritual in a circle may be needed, or not. There may be someone presiding over the event in a facilitator role, or not.

Then there are groups like Code Pink or the Clown Army transforming and playing with energies on the streets dressed in pink or wearing clown outfits. It is all about turning the status quo upside down – and it's not being done in the old dualistic 'them and us' way, in which the police or the government is being attacked. It is not about thinking that we are perfect and the authority must be destroyed. Rather it's about dissolving the hierarchies of inequality though transformation of energy and siding with the natural balancing mechanisms of nature. The energy of fear turns into mocking laughter. The authority is no longer frightening but absurd. The energy of rage is danced into action. Anger becomes creative.

The Underground Flow Beneath the City Streets

Deep under the concrete, rigidity of London's streets and skyscrapers, banks and courts, lie several lost rivers, symbols of a transgressive energy that has always flowed in the city. I first felt an urge to open up these blocked flows while meditating with a group in Canonbury tower, a strange, medieval building in North London. A woman came in from the street, distressed and almost incoherent. She talked of unblocking the spring under the tower. We calmed her down and as a psychotherapist I assumed she was talking about her blocked libido in a poetic but rather disturbed way! But it turned out that there was indeed a spring under Canonbury tower, now covered over like most of the old wells and springs of London. Driven by the feeling that they represented a more feminine and fluid energy desperately needed today, I began to research them. The best-known underground river, the Fleet, ended up filthy and polluted, now encased in a pipe and is still pouring into the Thames at Blackfriars. This was in spite of the architect Wren's plan to clean it up and turn it into a Venetian-style water way. I became especially fascinated with the Fleet as it rose in two main channels on Hampstead Heath curling round the ancient sacred mound of Parliament Hill where the ponds are now. I have even landed up living in a house on the banks of where it used to flow in Kentish Town.

Because of my feeling for this river, I have often taken students to the source of the Fleet near to Kenwood House where she flows out of the earth as red

Source of the River Fleet

water – or was it really her blood? She emerges in a forgotten marshy but sacred corner of the heath. We would honor 'her' by dipping our fingers in and making spirals on each other's foreheads.

Over the past 20 years I have visited sites all over the city, alone, with friends or as part of the Dionysian Underground, a Pagan Anarchist Group. Sometimes we do rituals or ceremonies with personal or political intentions. Sometimes we simply honor the forgotten spirits and energies of the place. A few sites are sacred to particular known goddesses or gods, such as the pre-Roman ones of Elen at St Helen's and Brigit at St Brides. These are churches on either side of the City of London. The once flowing energy between them is now blocked by one of the main financial centers of world capitalism Just as their financial systems block the sustainable rhythms of natural economics, so the actual buildings block the earth and water energies of the place. So reconnecting and invoking these forgotten goddesses hold special significance.

On May Day in 2004 a group of us decided to 'take on the city'. The Bank of England and the Stock Exchange looked brooding and dark, heavy and grim. Everywhere there were the pillars of patriarchal classical Greek temples, giving sacred power to the terrible perversion of earth energy that is a legacy of modern capitalism.

We had the intention to use the metaphor of the rivers and springs dissolving the rigid hierarchical structures of the city. We took with us a snake, symbol of the movement between opposites that moves the universe itself. The group gathered at St Brides. This church lies where the Fleet turns down towards the Thames on the site of an old sacred well. The exact spot of the well seems to be under modern drain. So we formed a circle around the drain. It seemed symbolic of what hierarchical control has done to the life force of the planet. We were there to set the rivers and springs free, in ourselves as well in the city. There we were, a motley crew, with masks, drums and colored umbrellas, reminiscent of a Vodou procession. We evoked the energies of the goddess Brigit, pagan ancestor of the saint, and visualized the well as it once was, surrounded by revelers and rebels, throwing flowers, dancing and making love. We drummed and chanted.

Then we set off up Ludgate Hill, offering apples to passers by, like Eve tempting others to tune into the transgressive energies of the land. Some smiled, some joined us and some simply looked bemused. Our next stop was outside St Pauls Cathedral. Another circle was formed with a statue of Artemis/Diana in the center. There had apparently once been a temple to her on the site. It was her wild huntress energies we evoked now to dismantle the solidity of the patriarchal religion represented there today.

We then stopped in the heart of the City at the Royal Exchange and Bank of England to raise more dissolving energy. The air felt heavy and dark. Some of us felt physically sick. But we chanted and laughed and sprinkled magic water everywhere. The energy seemed to change. We finally got to St Helen's at the end of the ley line. There we told each other stories about Elen ancient goddess of London. It was a peaceful spot underneath the towering monsters of glass and concrete. We talked about the consequences of capitalism and the lost power of Elen's healing, spiritual and revolutionary energy. I felt inspired at first and then suddenly very small and powerless. It seemed as though we sat for hours, meditating in that magic place overshadowed by the gigantic office blocks all around us. There were moments for me when it all felt so pointless. Then someone reminded us that every little action adds to the whole. It adds its energy as well as its physical impact. There is a river of energy and thought change happening in the world, and we are a part of it. Hope returned and we left seven apples in the churchyard and went home. The earth goddess Rhea or Gaia, has her own ways of rebalancing things.

What is different about this new, more spiritual protest movement, is a deep honoring and trusting of the earth and her natural balancing movements. Many activists have a profound respect for 'Gaia', as she is often called. For some it is not just respect, but what can only be described as a deep love.

A client we will call Sylvia had never felt really safe with her mother as a child. She was left in the care of unkind young nannies and developed a strong defensive wall around herself. No one could be trusted. That is, no human being could be trusted. Yet from an early age she found places in nature that were really safe. There was a big old oak tree at the end of their garden. It felt protective and Sylvia would spend hours in its branches reading, or sitting at its foot.

She would run away to the nearby beach and feel held by the landscape. It was as if the sea was her mother. Sylvia became an artist working with natural objects and treating them as sacred. She also became an activist, campaigning to stop roads being built over sacred land and lived in a homemade bender for many months. But she became very angry, at first mainly with the authorities who brought in the bulldozers. But then it was with everyone around her. She flew into rages at the slightest provocation. When she then became depressed Sylvia came to therapy. Much of the initial focus was on the sacredness of her own body and she did many paintings of herself for the first time. When her self love was strong enough, we worked on her relationship with her mother. The hurt and rage came pouring out. Then eventually came the acceptance of her mother's limitations and things as they actually are.

She became much more effective and powerful in her protest work, holding rituals to Gaia in front of the bulldozers. By doing the inner work, Sylvia could channel her valuable anger and her love better. She now had her own inner support. In therapy we also worked with invoking comforting images of Gaia for her to use when she was feeling depressed or lonely. Sylvia would picture herself sitting on the lap of great mother earth and being held in her arms.

Rhythms of Resistance
From the anarchists of the Spanish Civil war to the student protesters of the 1960s, rebels have always tried to develop processes of organization

based on equality, to match their ideals. These have often been misunderstood, despised as being too fluffy, chaotic or ineffective, or considered irrelevant to the main task of revolution. Yet they do have order, it is simply that that order is self regulating and not enforced from above. The shape that this self regulation takes is a rhythmic to-ing and fro-ing, between opposites. For example, power shifts backwards and forwards between groups and individuals. No one has it all the time. People tune in at different levels to the energies

Rhythmic Rebellion

and needs of the moment, and act accordingly, so there can be fluidity when things need changing. This way of organizing is described by Wilhelm Reich in *Natural Work Democracy*.[3] He argues that power hierarchies actually stop people attending to the practical needs of whatever task they are faced with.

In the 1970' a pamphlet called *The Tyranny of Structurelessness* was very popular amongst feminists and alternative socialists. The authors argued that if there is no structure at all for meetings and organizing actions and events, then the most confident individuals take over. Such informal structures could be even more hierarchical than the old socialist ones of majority rule. Feminists were especially aware that middle class white women often took charge or had greater influence than others. What happened next in the 1980s, was that the silenced groups split off. For example, black women formed their own groups. Identity politics based on one defining characteristic became the norm.

Today, beyond identity politics, what seems to be developing on the ground are different kinds of structures, fluid, flowing, rhythmic ones. Identity itself is experienced by many people as more fluid. The new protest politics is less rigidly identity based. Everyone can join the Pinks or the Greens. Meetings are usually in informal circles, with constantly shifting leadership, and to ensure a rhythmic structure in which people take turns respectfully, talking sticks are often used. A 'talking stick' is a baton which is passed around the group, allowing people to speak in turn, without being interrupted, as it must be held before a person can speak. Agendas are often written on the spot. Some anarchist groups specifically call themselves the 'horizontals' to make the point about this paradigm shift.

Leadership is either very much in the background, or is enacted in a less personal, egoistic style. A well-known example is Sub commander Marcos of the Mexican Zapatistas, who would always wear a mask, and deliberately underplay his role of leader. He related their particular struggle to those of all oppressed people everywhere, even including 'single mums' and 'struggling small businesses'. He famously said that 'we are all Zapatistas now!'

On the streets, during demonstrations there are many ways in which the new paradigm is being expressed literally as rhythmic. Samba bands that accompany many protest actions are using rhythm as a revolutionary sound and even consciously as a metaphor for the new paradigm. On their website, the London based Samba band, Rhythms of Resistance[4] say that they are about 'subverting and overturning the hierarchical dualities that shape our thinking under capitalism'. They add, 'These thought patterns structure our everyday lives and lock us into patterns of behavior which privilege duty above pleasure, work over play, society over nature, male over female, straight over gay, white over black. In contrast, carnival is fluid, plural and collective.'

As the anarchist Emma Goldman once said, 'It's not my revolution if I can't dance'. But dance is also a metaphor for the kinds of energy flows needed to dissolve the hierarchies of society. It's not just about reforming society, but about transforming it.

It is not so much about confronting the police, as simply not taking seriously the hierarchical paradigm that separates them and puts them above and in control of us. Boundaries and borders are to be played with, crossed and dissolved. Rhythms still have opposites and lines they flow around, but these are always changing according to the needs of the moment. This is not to deny the powers that police have to quell demonstrations, which are sometimes used brutally, for example in Genoa 2002.

The public march in London in February 2003, protesting against the Iraq war, was the biggest demonstration the city has ever known. But like so many smaller ones before and since, it was also different in the sheer variety of people taking part and in the fluid, rhythmic way so many groups treated the event. From the barrios of Brazil came the sounds of the Samba with their sexy beats stirring the more solemn marchers walking wearily along, chanting predictable slogans. With the bands came half naked boys and girls in silver and pink, dancing at first in lines. The music changed with the multi-cultural mix of the participants – turning into a circle dance joined by delighted Palestinians. As the circle dancers slipped down a side street away from the agreed route, shoppers moved their feet in tune with the beat – some even joined in. Spontaneous actions were sparked and shared on mobile phones.

Fiercely articulate Muslim woman wearing the hijab spoke from loudspeakers about the many different hierarchies being struggled against. Next to them, anxious 'Jews for Justice in Palestine' carried lists of the dead on both sides, acutely and uncomfortably aware of the irony of Holocaust victims having become the new persecutors. Then came the determined 'Older Feminists Against War', reminding everyone of the hierarchy of ageism, so often forgotten. Further along, a line of Buddhist monks were walking very slowly and smiling serenely, but present as witnesses to the crime of war. Then there were the banners boldly proclaiming 'Let's make tea not war'. A large circle was formed on the banks of the Thames and pagan priestesses in flowing black robes and jeans evoked the energies of Isis, goddess of the river. We called on her to use her transformative waters to dissolve the hardened hearts of parliament and to guide the flow of our protest march.

On another protest in Piccadilly Circus the Dionysian underground was staging an 'Eros against Capitalism' event. It seemed fun at first thought, but the sheer numbers of police and the wooden walls they had erected to protect Eros, terrified me. I had to concentrate hard and meditate deeply, to be fully in the flow and focus only on Eros. It soon became clear to everyone that this was a sacred ritual, not an attack. To my relief the police stood back as if in trance themselves, and the procession of masked Dionysian protesters in black, walked slowly through the crowd, beating a single drum. After what seemed like an eternity we reached the steps of the statue of Eros. Suddenly as if from nowhere, revelers in bright costumes surrounded us. We read out poetry and declaimed the appropriation of our natural eroticism by capitalism, as hundreds of cyclists from the radical group Critical Mass sped round Piccadilly Circus hooting and cheering.

Protesting is changing. Rebelling is changing. Politics is changing. The old ways no longer get to the deepest roots of the problems. The secular religion that worships the market and its greed for endless profit, cannot be counter-acted just by party politics and lawyers. A change is needed in the human psyche, a spiritual change that dissolves the hierarchies in our minds and hearts, a change that transforms them into ever flowing rhythms of loving rebellion. And underneath so many of these changes is a belief, often unconscious, often taken for granted, in deep human equality.

Is There an Equalizing Instinct?

A group of children in an African village are playing with a wooden stick and an old bicycle wheel being used as a hoop. It is the only toy they have. The bigger children make sure the younger ones all get a turn in rolling it along. Everyone gets a chance to play with it. On another continent girls are skipping in a concrete playground. They hold the rope for each other and encourage each one to succeed, singing and chanting as they go. Yet another group of Hopi children in a Native American village play ball, willing both sides to succeed. No one wins. Tourists on a Greek beach play bat and ball. The only aim is to keep the ball in the air. They can go on all day. All these humans are engaged in equalizing behavior. They are in the flow, and they all seem quite happy!

Was this behavior laboriously learnt through classes in good citizenship, or is there a part of us that naturally or even instinctively strives for equality when the circumstances allow it? 'Natural' is a very dangerous word. The whole idea of human nature has had very bad press over the last 30 or so years. So to suggest that there might be an equal-izing instinct is surely jumping in where angels fear to tread. But there is evidence from anthropology that many cultures, past and present, have not had any problems persuading their members towards equality. Native American tribes, like the Hopi, were described by early settlers as working and sharing as equals, despite differences in their social functions. This shocked the hierarchical Europeans. The Cherokee in the 18th Century were described critically by white people as 'having no law or subjugation between them... the very lowest of them thinks himself as great and high as any of the rest.' Shock, horror! In such societies there is actually shame attached to having too much more than anyone else. Generosity is praised over greed or superiority. Fear of envy is stronger than the desire to win. Equality comes more easily than competitiveness.

Meanwhile, in the modern world, everywhere we look there is compe-tition. Each time we switch on the TV there is some kind of contest, to be a millionaire or to stay in the Big Brother house. This win-or-lose paradigm sinks deep into our unconscious minds. Imagine us living in an equalizing world like that of the Hopi. Picture yourself watching football on TV with friends. When your team scores a goal, everyone roars with joy. When the other team scores there's a groan of disappointment. But what if the approval came whenever there was an equalizing goal, whenever the teams evened up... Imagine people hugging each other every time equality was achieved!

While egalitarian tribal societies are relatively rare in the world today, there is evidence from archaeology as described by Steve Taylor in *The Fall*, that in most densely inhabited areas before about 4000 BC 'inequality and social oppression was largely absent'. As modern humans have been around for about 150,000 years it, seems that for the first 144,000 years or more of our existence, we had the capacity to live in relatively equal groups. It clearly gave us an evolutionary advantage. As we haven't changed physically in all that time, it is likely that any instincts we had then, we still have now. So it must be that humans still have the potential to live more equally. This potential is simply buried under heavy layers of learnt ideologies and inner structures of power and status, competition and hierarchy. And to keep these layers in place, there is another primal instinct, fear. Only strong and loving rebellion can counteract it. Deep rebellion seems to come out of an equalizing instinct. But there are different kinds of rebellion.

When a person or group is simply reacting against an authority within a dualistic framework, that authority maintains a hold over the so-called rebel. All too often the rebel simply ends up becoming the next, even stricter authority. But Wilheim Reich the radical psychotherapist, argues that this kind of limited rebellion does not come from the deepest core of the self. Rebellion that comes from a deeper equalizing instinct is different. He writes that, 'Everything that is genuinely revolutionary, every genuine art and science, stems from man's biological core... Since the break down of the primitive work-democratic form of social organization, the biologic core of man has been without social representation ... and being revolutionary (is) the rational rebellion against intolerable conditions in human society...' Rebellion can be seen as a necessary mutation from the norm, for evolutionary progress. If humans had always accepted the status quo or simply replaced it, we would still be in the

Stone Age. And as individuals, too, we don't evolve unless we rebel.

A client we shall call Pauline came from a poor working class background. Various impulses drove her to be the opposite. Rebelling against her parents was her first step. Wanting to equalize with the middle classes was second step. Never again did she want to go without the designer clothes of her classmates, or their big toys at Christmas. It was the social shame and sense of inferiority that mattered more than the actual objects. Pauline put herself through university studying law, with the help of an older man who supported her. She hated herself for sleeping with him but was too driven to notice. Pauline worked her way up through the law firm to become a partner. She had a beautiful apartment, beautiful clothes and a beautiful car. Then at the age of 35 she fell in love with a 26 year old human rights lawyer. This was a rebellion against the sexual mores of the society. He changed her thinking dramatically and persuaded her to go with him to Africa and work for an aid agency. This third step involved her in the desire to equalize the massive inequalities of the wider world. At first Pauline was happy. Life seemed more meaningful and she was in love. But the old hole of inferiority returned and she gave more and more of her power away to her partner, who had come from a wealthy background. She resented the way it was easier for him to give up what he had owned because he had grown up with money. So she rebelled against him by arguing and crying, raging and sulking. Pauline eventually left him, thinking she needed to return to her old life. All those ideals had been pointless. Africa was in a mess, she was powerless, and what's more, she had only made herself miserable and poor, just like her mother.

At this point she came to therapy and began to develop a stronger sense of her core self. She began to rebel against the empty, secular nature of the society. Pauline became interested in paganism and in the deep equalizing processes in nature itself. She began to celebrate the phases of the moon and the seasons, and to meditate and live more in the flow. When she was able to be in the flow, her intuition was clear and she was not simply reacting from deep inferiority. Up until this point, much of her rebellion had been reactive rather than coming from the depths of her core self. She was locked into a paradigm of inferior working class and superior middle class. Her rebellion had stayed within the system. When she contacted her core self and became attuned to the flow she could step right outside the hierarchical mind set. Pauline took time to find the right work and eventually found a law firm that helped the disadvantaged. She was working from a different place of love as well as an acute awareness of injustice.

While the research has not been done to prove an equalizing instinct, we can see that psychotherapists such as Reich have argued for it in the past. Anthropologists and archaeologists have demonstrated its presence in hundreds of past and present human societies. So if we do have an innate desire to equalize, how can we recognize it, develop it and express it more effectively? And how can we differentiate between healthy, loving rebellion from the core of ourselves, and a more superficial, defensive kind caught up in the old authoritarian structures?

The Inner Rebel

We hear a lot about 'working with the inner child' but it's now time to get to know our 'inner rebel' too. It is well known to parents and psychologists that around the age of two lots of children start rebelling against the authority of parents or siblings. It is often a time of power struggle where the tiny little person begins to assert her or his autonomy, willpower and sense of fairness and equal rights. Then, as teenagers and young adults, many of us rebel against some authority or another. It is usually aimed towards parents, and then at teachers, the police or even the whole culture in which they live. This may be more common in some societies than others. Anthropologists like Margaret Mead show us that it is not universal, but it is a very widespread phenomena in the modern western world. It is likely that aspects of this rebellion are necessary psychologically for the child and young adult to develop a sense of their separate self. 'Finding oneself' is a basic demand today, whether by going on a trip round the world, refusing an arranged marriage or dropping out of college. Just how separate and individual the young person is expected to be depends on the culture. But rebellion may be a necessary part of 'becoming a person'. This could be described as (1) 'developmental rebellion'.

Another kind of rebellion, often mixed in with 'developmental rebellion' is the kind that Reich describes, which is (2) 'authoritarian rebellion' against any authority – simply because it is an authority. Ironically it is a way of staying connected to that authority. There is no genuine freedom to make clear and appropriate choices. It all has to be anti this or anti that. It is trapped in the dualism.

The third kind is (3) 'loving rebellion', which emerges from the equalizing instinct in our deepest core. It comes from a sense of gross injustice or simply an everyday urge to equalize wherever possible. It also comes from the freedom to act appropriately without our defenses, ego, pride or fear.

My daughter was a very rebellious teenager, towards me as a parent, towards teachers and towards society as a whole. Some of this was a necessary part of developmental rebelliousness, some was understandable rage against a racist world, but she also expressed some very deep loving rebelliousness. I took her and a friend to the Gambia on a 'cheap' package holiday one summer when she was 14. We stayed in a luxury hotel, while outside on the beach, armed police were stationed to protect the tourists from the many ragged children who tried to eke out a living selling crafts. She was so enraged by this inequality that after befriending several of the children she brought them into the hotel, round the swimming pool and up to the bar where they were all sat on high stools and bought drinks. It was an act that came from her core, a little act of loving rebellion.

Many of us carry out these 'little' acts of loving rebellion every day of our lives, often without thinking about them. When we deliberately talk to the unattractive woman or man in the corner at a party, we are engaging in an act of equalization. In any group, giving space and time to the less confident or shy person is equalizing. It may even involve ignoring the over-confident man in the suit! Choosing partners or friends from different classes or ethnic backgrounds can be a form of equalizing for millions in the modern world. The grandfather who takes out the garbage or washes up after a meal may be trying to equalize in his own way, as is the teenager who gives up his seat to an older person on a bus. Of course the context matters. For a couple who have been working on a basis of equality for years, doing the washing up would hardly be a big deal. But for someone brought up to expect women to do all the dirty work, it would be a gesture of equalizing.

A client we will call Thomas was brought up by a very strict Afro Caribbean family. When his parents came to Britain from the West Indies in the 1960s they were quietly disappointed by the casual racism they faced each day. Putting a brave face on the limited opportunities they were given, the local black church became their main support. The bible was read every day at the breakfast, lunch and supper tables. Punishments for the children's childish crimes were all carried out in the name of the Lord. Thomas hated his father.

As soon as he could leave home, Thomas left. With the support of his girlfriend from a similar background, he went to college, did media studies and created his own music production company. His rage at authority in general and at the racism he experienced on the street in particular, was expressed in the lyrics of the music he wrote. Thomas became a street rapper with a following of disillusioned youth. But he was consumed with the anger and his loyal long-term girlfriend eventually threatened to leave. At this point he did a course on anger management, which helped him manage his emotional outbursts. But Thomas was still locked into the hierarchical dualism of them and us. By being so relentlessly anti any authority he was actually internally imprisoned by that very authority. In therapy he began to think differently, firstly about himself. By taking his own internal authority and loving himself more he could step back from the exhausting battle that had taken over his life. His rebellion was transformed, not destroyed. It now came from his strong core self and was a reaction to real injustice and real racism. He started a radio station to give positive inspiration to black youth. The lyrics of his songs also changed.

Equalizing is not only about bringing others 'up' – it can also be about bringing ourselves 'up'. Assertiveness is all about equalizing. When we look our boss in the eye as an equal human being and refuse to be put down or intimidated, we are equalizing. Equality does not mean sameness. Some people are better at playing the piano than others. This does not make them fundamentally superior human beings.

Then there are the 'bigger' inequality issues, like world poverty. People on all sides of the political spectrum sometimes feel revulsion, from the core of their being, at the massive inequalities in the world. These can seem like such enormous problems that we feel powerless. But there are always small but meaningful actions that can be taken. These might include campaigning. For other people the actions might involve their own life choices, such as downsizing to live more simply, buying fair trade goods, or sharing a car. Even giving to charities, which is often rather despised by the left, is a way that some people make an effort to equalize, putting their investment into a charity's campaign for a better deal for farmers or fairer justice. In that place of deepest intuition, most of us feel uncomfortable with massive inequalities when we are really forced to face them. It's only on the more superficial level of our defenses, ego and pride that we buy into the admiration of celebrity, material possessions and status that runs our world today. And when we are reasonably empty of all those issues, we can hear our intuition, inner wisdom or core self. Then, and only then, we are truly in the flow. And then we tend to naturally desire to equalize, in whatever situations we find ourselves.

All the major religions speak about equality and justice somewhere in their writings. Most spiritual leaders have a remarkable humility. They can sense that every human is valuable in some way, even if their actions are not. And when we are in the flow we can see this equality clearly. In this place loving rebellion becomes natural.

Deepak Chopra[5] wrote that 'Nature abhors a deep imbalance'. As we have seen, the flow is itself a rhythmic, equalizing process, known as enantiodromia by the ancient Greeks and the Tao by the ancient Chinese. This can be seen as the spirit in matter. By attuning ourselves to this balancing force we are actually harmonizing with nature.

When we support the underdog in an unjust situation we are in touch with nature's deepest rhythms. Whether the underdog is the bullied child in the school playground or a whole group of people, they are all being treated as lesser in some way. In one context this could be Jewish people, in another Palestinians. In one context it could be women and in another gay men. In one context it could be Muslims, in another Christians. But loving rebellion is not the same as knee jerk revenge or action based on envy. It comes from a different part of ourselves. Any loving action we take to equalize is spiritual in the sense of attuning to unseen flowing energies. When we refuse to fight in an occupying army we are attuned to the spirit in matter. When we refuse to listen to racist jokes we are connecting to the spirit in matter. When we rage against injustice, cry in sympathy with the tortured, scream at the sky for the horror of war, we become spirit in matter itself.

Things to do: Becoming Aware of your History of Rebelling
1. Look at your own personal history of rebelling. Draw a lifeline starting from birth, showing where rebellious times or specific acts of rebellion occurred. Then decide which kind of rebellion it was developmental, authoritarian or loving.

2. Look at your life situation right now. Does it need more or less rebellion? What might be blocking you, being in touch with your core, loving, rationally rebelling self? Is there a recent situation in which you would have liked to rebel, but didn't? What stopped you?

3. Draw your inner rebel. What does she, he or it look like. What do

they want to say to you right now?

4. Think about meetings or groups that you are a part of. Are there practical ways in which you could encourage a more equalizing structure? Could you put chairs into a circle instead of straight rows? Could you rotate the chairperson so someone different leads each meeting? Could you suggest that everyone has a chance to speak? Can you identify, value and use the specific abilities of each member, bearing in mind that equality does not mean sameness,?

5. Try emptying your mind of all the hierarchical ego defenses for one day, and notice how you react in social situations. Be aware of times when you were not free, where you didn't tune in to the needs of the moment. What stopped you? What was different about the times when you did tune in? If emptying the mind is really hard (as it is for all of us) try practicing meditating on the rhythm of the breath, saying quietly 'in' and 'out'. Maybe it is especially hard because your mind is so full of stuff. What do you think are your main psychological issues? What would help you deal with them?

6. Take any political problem, and work out which different hierarchies are involved. First brain storm and see just how many you can think of. Then look at which ones are to the fore and which are in the background. Which ones are very large inequalities with enormous gaps between the tops and bottoms, and which ones are smaller? Draw a diagram of all the hierarchies and a wavy line to show where change is needed. Which ones can you do something about changing? What actions by others, such as governments or corporations could be carried out to change them? How can you support or encourage those actions?

CHAPTER FOUR

DANCING THE RHYTHM OF LIFE

The word 'equality' can sound like a very boring thing associated with dreary committee rooms and complex burocracy. This stereotyped image needs to be changed. Instead it can be seen as an exciting, dramatic process, equalizing between opposites of all kinds from masculine and feminine to positive and negative magnetic poles. It can be likened to a dance, a force pushing and pulling towards and away from opposites, whether between human individuals or between electrons and protons in the atom. Equalizing rhythms flowing between opposites create the life force itself. This energetic to-ing and fro-ing was the role of the Greek God Eros and of his female counterpart Era. In the deepest meaning of the word, equalizing rhythms are erotic. Equality can be sexy.

A couple called Bob and Cathy came for therapy because their sex lives had become boring. They loved each other very much and wanted children. But Cathy could not get pregnant. She pretended not to care about this, as her career was the main focus of her life. They described various efforts that they had made to spice things up a bit, they had tried some dominance and submission with whips and handcuffs. But they ended up giggling too much. Neither of them felt really turned on in either role. Instead we worked on raising sexual energy in their bodies first, using various techniques such as squeezing certain muscles. Then they meditated together emptying their minds and following the energy wherever it led them. Neither partner was in charge. No one was dominating yet in a sense they were both surrendering their wills to the energy itself. They soon found themselves fully in the flow and discovered a powerful eroticism way beyond all expectations. Within days Cathy was pregnant.

Equality often works better than domination in everyday sexuality.

Being in the flow is more fun, more ecstatic and more intense than mechanically controlling what happens. Orgasm is itself uncontrollable rhythms that take us over. We can't help but be attuned to them. Imagine living one's whole life in that attunement to endless inner and outer rhythms. And beyond individual ecstatic attunement, imagine whole communities tuned in together.

In this chapter we look at three main areas, where at least for a short space of time, millions of ordinary people are dissolving hierarchies and tuning into the rhythms of life collectively. The first of these is through rave culture. The second is through carnival. And the third is through connecting with the rhythms of nature and paganism in particular.

Rave Against the Grave

'In the end, there is only the dance.' I heard these words loud and clear in my head one night recently, while waking from a dream. I thought, 'Wow! That is it! Rhythm philosophy in a nutshell.' It means that matter/energy is dancing at every level and in every dimension. As a child I had danced to the drums of local tribes in southern Sudan. From then on, I would take any opportunity to dance, anywhere, to anything. But there was a freedom about rave culture that especially appealed to me. I started going to raves in the early 1990s when I was already in my forties. At first I went with a deep inner hierarchy of ageism, which made me feel self conscious among all those beautiful young bodies. Yet I sensed that something powerfully, culturally transformative and of universal importance was happening here. What was it? My hippie days were long past, but some of that revolution in consciousness was back here. Those tiresome inner hierarchies were soon dissolved in the beats that took me over. Everyone was just dancing in their own way. They were not competing or choosing partners, as least not in an obvious way. I was as much a part of the dance as anyone else. Soon I was transported into an ecstatic loss of ego, and of any fears I originally had. Eventually I would literally dance all night without the help of drugs or even coffee. This was for me a profoundly spiritual experience. And I could dance exactly how I wanted to, giving myself up to the flow. There was indeed a sense of deep equality, with some raves increasingly aligning themselves specifically with equalizing politics.

In 2002, 4,000 young people in Israel attended a 'Rave against the Grave' in Jerusalem. It was not the kind of spiritual event normally held in that ancient, religious city. But in its own way it was a kind of political/spiritual happening. The organizers had set out their mission on the website Peacecoalitionumbrella.org: 'We can no longer bear the distortion of human values in our society. We want life not death. This war is not ours and we should get out of the occupied territories.'[1] But rather than demonstrate on the streets in the old style, they chose to party for peace. Can this approach actually change anything? Is something new and radical beginning to stir under the rectangular tables of brutal negotiations and the sad streets of endless shopping? It seems as though there is an alternative global youth culture developing not just on Indian beaches but also in the African bush, not just in commercial clubs but in disused warehouses everywhere. But does it actually threaten the status quo at all? Or is it just a bit of fun for the rich kids to let off steam at weekends before returning on Mondays to support the system in corporate jobs?

Young men do say that the energy they express in raves stops them acting aggressively outside. Only a few authorities have utilized this connection. For example, in Luton, UK in 2001, the local council put on free weekly raves. The crime rate was more than halved, during that time. But since the beginnings of the rave scene in the late 1980s most authorities have cracked down on the whole culture, unless it is purely commercial. They see it as a threat. Are they seeing something that the rest of us don't?

In Britain The Criminal Justice Bill in 1994 actually specified limiting the playing of *repetitive beats*. The demonstration against the bill in London included floats with sound systems, that are now banned on marches in London. What can be so threatening about repetitive beats, about rhythm? It seems that by attuning to rhythms and reaching states of ecstasy people get more in touch with their deepest intuition. And when they are more deeply intuitive they can see the emptiness of society's values and the injustice of inequalities. At many raves there are stalls and film shows about injustice in the world. These speak directly to those who are conscious of their political motivations, but they may have an impact on partygoers subconsciously too. Rhythm on one level can lead to rhythm thinking on another.

For many people who go to raves, the political dimension feels a million miles away. But it may be that the power of rhythm sinks deep into the unconscious, to open the intuition and experience a connectedness with others and nature that is preparing them for a totally different kind of society. So while the activists are still a very small minority, it may be that the equalizing influences on mainstream culture are not so much through party politics, newspapers or even TV. There may be a more subtle effect, through the rave culture. Raves or parties, and the related alternative festivals like Synergy in the UK and The Burning Man in the US, are some of the main places where the radical, rhythm model is actually being lived. The organizers even try to be as non hierarchical as they can, creating collectives where possible.

Is Dance Culture a New Spirituality?

'God is a DJ. Life is a dance floor, Love is the rhythm.' Pink (2003)

In a Raver's Manifesto of 2001, rhythms were described at the 'heart beat of Gaia'. As people tune into her heartbeat they also synchronize with each other. If tuning into rhythms of nature and of each other is what defines spirituality, it can be a genuine spiritual experience. With or without mind-altering drugs, people often experience a sense of resonating with rhythms at very high vibrations. These are states that can take years of conventional meditation to reach. Rhythmic beats have been used by most human cultures for thousands of years to achieve trance like states. And these states have been used for 'seeing' into the future, giving advice or for a whole variety of ways of helping the society. They help to develop intuitive powers. And we have already noted that the old hierarchies and ego states dissolve when we are in touch with our deepest intuition. Our wisdom then is 'clean'. We see things as they are.

A client called John aged 48 came to therapy for mild depression and a sense of pointlessness in life. His wife of 20 years had left him for another woman. He felt unattractive and lonely. Various attempts at speed dating had left him feeling worse than before. He had an air of desperation. Instead of focusing on his lack we explored his experiences as a young man in meditation where he had reached states of ecstasy more and more often as he continued to practice. He was a highly intuitive man who had long ago stopped trusting that part of himself. All that was given up when he married, as his wife was quite materialistic and contemptuous of his spiritual side. In the therapy we started to meditate together and I would 'take him on imaginary journeys' to 'find' his lost sides. This was combined with a deepening of his trust in me, and his own work on mourning his lost relationship. John was very angry with women at first. After a year of work he started going to raves of the alternative kind. He rediscovered his lost 'inner hippie' and relaxed into the ecstatic experience. He was no longer searching for the perfect woman, or eying up the young ones with frustrated longing. His bruised ego began to dissolve. He became a much-loved member of the community, even joining the collective that was organizing the raves/parties. Eventually he met a woman who was similar to himself and began to live more in the flow in his everyday life.

These altered states of consciousness do seem to help people begin to let go of the ego. The sense of a separate, special, superior self is a hierarchical concept. Dissolving this ego with others in a rave helps with the important spiritual task of letting it go in life generally. Ecstasy translates from the Greek, as 'being outside of the self or ego'. In that state we can be in the flow, attuned to many different rhythms and vibrations. Ego self-consciousness blocks our ability to be in the flow. The flow, as we have seen, is the equalizing rhythm of energy between any sets of opposites. It can be a very fast vibration that takes us to other dimensions, or the unseen force balancing high and low in human culture. But when in the flow, it is our deepest intuition that guides us, not superficial reason. As Mihaly Csikszentmohalyi[2] wrote, people enter a flow state when the ego falls away, time flies, and every movement and thought follows inevitably from the previous one. Your whole being is involved. He likens it to playing jazz. But it is also like the experience of being in a rave.

Spiritual Imagery

We also tend to have more peak experiences when in the flow. These are described by humanistic psychologists like John Rowan[3], and can be seen as moments of attunement to perfect rhythm. We are synchronizing with the universe itself. We are not thinking with the logical mind, but attuning to the deeper *logos* of the endlessly balancing cosmos. And many of the visual effects used in raves help the process of attuning and letting go of the ego. There are often overtly spiritual images around the rave scene. Pagan pentacles, Hindu and Buddhist gods and goddesses are found everywhere. But so are images of aliens, crop circles and fractals endlessly swirling into space. Even the Techno raves have a spiritual feel, as if the music and visuals are tuning in to pure abstract rhythm itself. Many rave organizations, like Synergy are consciously creating a common culture of environmental and social sustainability. They are harnessing the powers of celebration to create social change. At Synergy the rave starts with an opening circle ritual. At Megatripolis, a regular rave event set up in the 1990s by Frazier Clarke who was one of the first to intentionally include spirituality, some of us would meditate in the club before everyone else arrived.

Graham St John[4] has gone even further in editing a book titled *Rave*

Culture and Religion. I prefer to use the term spirituality rather than religion. In the rave culture there are no sacred books, no unquestionable dogmas, and no policy of exclusion. And there is not so much of a star, celebrity system as in other areas of the music world. Of course hierarchies do creep in. Some might argue that DJs are seen as high priests or even gods, as in the Pink lyrics, or the Faithless track *God is a DJ*. But hierarchical structures are not part of the core belief system, so it is not strictly a new religion, it's more of a new spirituality.

There is also a healing element in rave culture. More and more parties include areas for meditation, massages or reflexology. There can be a rhythm between dancing and chilling out, being active and resting. It can feel natural for some people to do both, rather than determinedly dance all night, non-stop. Each person comes with their own imbalances that a rave can heal. Like the young men mentioned earlier, many people need to let out raging energy in a safe place. Others need to feel a sense of community. But the sound of repetitive beats itself can be healing on an energy level. We have different vibrations in different parts of our bodies, and in different organs. If these become sluggish or speeded up, or simply out of tune, the sound and sight of rhythms can realign them. An external rhythm synchronizing with a messed up internal rhythm can bring it back into a healthy flow.

There is a spirituality in music that connects across all religious and ethnic divides. Today as well as the dance movement, there is an ever-expanding global culture of mixing different styles of music together, acoustic & electronic. Many events include rave music and live bands. And there are usually people from all ethnic backgrounds, classes and ages at a festival or rave. The rhythm unites people. Hierarchies divide. Rhythms of love in the rave clubs replace the hierarchies of fear and aggression that dominate drinking bars. The philosophy and intention is deep equality. And that is helped by equalizing rhythms at all levels and in all zones of participation, in the music as well as in the relationships between people.

Carnival Rhythms

I have been going to the Notting Hill Carnival in London almost every year since the early 1970s. There is a freedom and equality on those streets that satisfies some deep longing in me to live differently, more rhythmically. It

Carnival in the Streets

is an ecstatic experience, whether I'm dressing up, following a band or just milling about, on my own or with friends. Carnival seems to remind us somehow of what we humans have lost, over the past 5,000 years or so of hierarchical ways of living.

Yet, throughout written history, from ancient Rome to Medieval France, from the Caribbean to Brazil, there has usually been a carnival of some kind taking place at a particular time each year. It was a time when people could let off steam and turn the status quo upside down. In Rome, during the Saturnalia festival in late December, slaves were served by their masters. This was apparently in memory of the past, when people were more equal. Everyone had a holiday. Rich and poor alike celebrated with feasting, giving each other presents, and decorating temples with greenery, including holly. In fact it was rather like the Christian Christmas!

The best-known carnivals today were originally based on the Catholic calendar. They occur just before Lent, when luxuries are traditionally given up until Easter, allowing a final burst of pleasure before restriction sets in. Carnivals in the Caribbean and South America also developed as a form of protest against the prevailing political power structures. As a mass experience in many countries, carnival is now mainstream. It is a massive, society wide transformation of hierarchy into rhythm at least for a few days. Describing the Trinidad carnival Cy Grant[5] puts it beautifully. 'Carnival reflects the energy repressed ... It became the vehicle of protest against, and mockery of, a dominant order and repressive church... It is essentially a life giving ritual, the redemptive dance in the barren cities of rationalism and materialism.'

He also describes the steel pan, which is a vital feature of carnival in Trinidad as representing another kind of transformation from one state to its opposite. The oil drums left behind by the Western exploitation of local resources and people, were changed into instruments of magical rhythms. They were burnt and beaten into shapes that now create beautiful and complex sounds. This transformation is a kind of alchemical process from a base metal to the gold of heaven! As Cy Grant notes, 'The vibrations from the steel drums resonate with those of the universe itself.' The sound alone can cause ecstatic states, just like the repetitive beats of rave music. 'Everyone needs a sense of ecstasy.' There is a Dionysian feel to this carnival music, echoing the ancient festivals of Crete and of other more feminine and egalitarian societies. During carnival we can get a glimpse of how it might have been in those societies and how it still could be for us in the future.

During carnival, the oppressed worker can become a king, the shy woman can become a brazen courtesan, a bullied child is transformed into a princess. Everyone can be the opposite of what they are in normal life. In Venice and other European carnivals, the mask is a vital part of the play. Everyone can be someone else for a day. This fluid change of identity is itself rhythmic. People can move in carnival from one role to another and then back again in the space of hours. The usual status hierarchies no longer exist. You do not know who that masked beauty flirting with you, really is. She could be a grandmother. But it does not matter. You no longer need total identification with the ego. It's ok to flirt openly with a grandmother. You don't care what others think. On spiritual paths, people spend lifetimes trying to reach such states of fluidity and non-identification with the ego.

The idea of constantly shifting identities is also a popular post-modern idea. Imagine living all the time in such rhythmic flux, still feeling a core of being, but not permanently identified with one role or another! The carnival has been used as a metaphor for this more fluid way of being by post-modernists like Mikhail Bakhtin[6]. He takes very seriously the inversion of hierarchies and quotes the famous Taoist Lao Tzu, saying, 'What is high becomes low, and what is low becomes high'.

One set of opposites that he turns upside down are those of high and low culture. He brings what is generally seen as low culture, like carnival itself, into 'highbrow' academic discussions. He values play, humor, mimicry and mockery as transgressing against the status quo, in profound ways.

In everyday life, the same play can happen within our minds. It may only be where there is a massive political or economic power difference, where the underdogs need to assert themselves for survival, that such identities are important. For example, the Palestinians may need to stress their national identity in the present situation of such inequality.

The point of carnival is that everything is always changing, especially identities. There is no room for being stuck in just one. And in everyday life there is real danger when only one identity of a person is seen, as opposed to any other. In extreme circumstances this can say lead to a situation like Northern Ireland. A person may identify as a Protestant in contrast to Catholics. It could even lead to believing that all Catholics are evil and deserve killing. Young men, brainwashed in this way, actually admitted on TV to acting on that belief alone. Terrible crimes all over the world have followed from such extreme one-sided identities.

In contrast, Carnival asserts our common humanity underneath all the masks. We are all in vulnerable bodies that can dance, desire, have sex, get drunk, get sick and die. No one, however rich or 'important' can escape both the beauty and the absurdity of the human body. Anyone and everyone can make a fool of themselves during carnival. In fact during carnival the Fool is in charge. The fool leaps in where angels fear to tread.

In the carnival-esque approach to life there is no respect for hierarchies. People are essentially, profoundly equal. Those in power will be mocked. In Trinidad, during carnival the Calypsonians sing songs of witty and playful criticism and even downright insult about their leaders. It is a time the oppressed can uncover the truths about the Emperor's new clothes. Things can be seen as they really are.

Caribbean Rhythms

Carnival in Trinidad and London

Many of the steel bands like the Desperados started out coming from the rambling shanty towns high on the hills above the neat towns below. Coming down onto the streets, taking over the streets, making exciting, energetic, even angry music on the streets can feel like a revolutionary act in itself. The bands loudly proclaim that for today we are the masters. Young men, old men, and increasingly women stand up there on the floats beating their hearts out on the drums, high above the road. The old lorries that pull them so very slowly, have a dignity that day. In the past nice middle class boys were not allowed anywhere near those lorries. Now of course it is often glossier, bigger and more expensive. In Trinidad the whole country stops for the day. But the old rebellious magic is still there in the back streets before and after the grand parades.

The Trinidad carnival has been transported to many places, from

Toronto to New York but the carnival in Notting Hill, London is one of the largest. It is billed as the biggest party in Europe. From a time when a dozen steel bands each followed by a few dancers wandered the streets wherever the whim took them, it became a highly organized event. Now there are hundreds of bands, followed by hundreds of costumed mass players and massive, booming sound systems. At one time it was a chance for the marginalized Afro Caribbean community to show themselves to the world. This was, at last an opportunity to take over the streets, not only with music but with traditional food and of course the inevitable flow of rum and Caribbean beer too.

The white community used to stand and watch, like tourists being entertained by an exotic culture. But over the years more and more white, brown and black people from all over Europe have come to dress up, dance, and even to play pan. Pan is taught in many schools all over the world now, and has become a feature of mainstream society in many countries including Britain.

On carnival morning, the music blares out from a church hall, which is one of the many places in which the costumes have been made. Large tubs of goat stew and rice and peas are being presided over by efficient and bossy, older women. Crowds of supporters and players are milling around, eating and drinking. Passionate older men in costume are trying to organize the mass players, who keep straying off to talk on mobile phones or fix their costumes. It's time to start and everyone must be in place. The pan players take their positions. A latecomer arrives out of breath and is shouted at with gusto. There is a buzz of excitement in the air. At last the signal is given to go, and amid the sweet, fury of the steel pans and the urgency of whistle blowing, they are off. Young women wearing almost nothing but gold thongs and sequins start to wind their bodies to the beat, engrossed in the rhythm, oblivious to the lusty onlookers. Older women wind their waists with complete sexual abandon into the crotches of equally free young men. Two of them are practically horizontal on the road, while others clap and dance around them. Children in prams wave flags. The band with the costumed mass players is more than a hundred strong. Sometimes it moves fast to make space for floats coming behind, Sometimes they come to a complete halt as the bands in front meet a crossroads. Sometimes the sound systems playing Soca or hip hop drown out the sounds of pan. Flasks of rum are passed through the band. All are lost in the rhythm, in charge of the roads for a day. Private cars are banished, people power reigns supreme. Even the advertising that now pays for much of carnival is either subverted or ignored, for a day.

Carnival in the Mediterranean

There are still carnivals in Mediterranean countries that are survivals from ancient societies. Many of these may come from the pagan spring festivals that used dance and ritual to ensure the coming of fertile energy back to the land. An old form of carnival on the island of Gozo, next to Malta, has survived for centuries but is now being tidied up for the tourist trade. However in some towns, the real carnival takes place in the narrow alleyways behind the main square, in the margins, outside the mainstream. That is where carnival cannot be controlled and sanitized. It still mocks the hierarchies of church and state, and still involves drinking, dancing and dressing up, and cross dressing, men dressing up as women, is another way the opposites are played with, turning upside down the gender hierarchies, and starting a rhythmic fluidity to sexual identity.

Cross dressing is also a popular feature of the ancient goat carnivals remaining in remote parts of Greece. On the island of Skyros, before lent, some young men dress up as women. Others are in baby goat skins, with belts of large bells round their waists. They drink a lot and dance up to the monastery on a hill above the town. It is thought by some scholars to have been built over a temple to Dionysus. This may be the closest we have today to the old Dionysian spring festival. As one young man told me in a bar there one night, he feels as though he actually is the god when wearing the goat skins on carnival days. He becomes Dionysus. By actually embodying the god, they completely lose their normal identity, for a while. It is another ecstatic experience.

The day after carnival anywhere in the world can feel almost tragic. The streets are strewn with the remains of magnificent costumes tattered in the breeze, bare wires stick out through the dusty glitter like the broken bones of a dead animal. Months of laborious preparation is all for just a few hours of glory. But this does not bother the carnival players. This flow between the opposites of peak and decline, ecstasy and ordinariness, feasting and fasting is in tune with the rhythm of life itself. It is far removed from the addictive modern world that most of us live in today. There is no rhythm to the endless dissatisfaction, the pursuit of whatever it is one is addicted to... alcohol, cigarettes, food, sex, and the endless pursuit of profit. We have lost the art of living rhythmically. Carnival and its transformation into ordinariness, maybe one of the few models left of an attitude to life that permeated human societies and thinking for thousands of years.

Pagan Rhythms of Nature

Paganism has been brought to the forefront of Western culture with Harry Potter books and films, *Sabrina the Teenage Witch* and *Buffy the Vampire Slayer* on television and the popular widespread celebration of Halloween. It may be one of the main ways in which tuning into rhythmic energies in nature is entering the main stream.

The word pagan comes from the Latin 'paganni' used to describe the less 'civilized', country people who had kept their own spiritualities. Today there is a mass revival of what can loosely be called neo-paganism. The word is used to cover a very wide range of different ancient spiritualities from the earliest Palaeolithic times to the hierarchical pagan religions of the Roman empire. No one living in those times would have called themselves pagan. They would have been worshippers of Venus or Dionysus, people doing rituals that have become traditional celebrations. The one feature they all seem to have in common is the emphasis on attunement to the rhythms of nature. Moon and sun cycles are usually central, even in the more complex pagan religions.

The word 'pagan' is also used to describe a whole set of ideas and rituals that were largely developed in the West, in the 19th and 20th Centuries – individuals claiming connections with witches of the past, or 'channelled' information set up pagan groups such as the order of the Golden Dawn of which the poet Yeats was a member.

Paganism has often been used as a term of abuse by those of the biblical religions. In their hierarchical frameworks it is often labelled as inferior, seen in opposition to the 'pure' religions of Islam, Judaism and Christianity. It is even associated with evil, the devil or the darkness that existed before the 'enlightened' new religion. There is a vertical relationship between light at the top, and the lower, dangerous, pagan dark. This paradigm remains today, even though witches are no longer burnt at the stake in most countries. It is important for us to reclaim the rhythmic spirituality that tunes in to the flow between light and dark. It does not separate them and pitch one in battle with the other, as in God versus Satan. Of course some pagans have taken this to absurd lengths by only concentrating on the 'dark' side to counteract Christianity's overemphasis on the victory of the light. But a lifetime's commitment to being a Goth or to endlessly practicing satanic rituals could be a bit depressing.

Most pagans are much more into the rhythmic balancing of opposites. The dark side is a part of life and within every one of us. It needs to be explored, psychologically, in dream and shamanic work. But the ultimate aim is balance. The website of the London Pagan Federation[7] describes its main principles. The first is 'Love for and kinship with nature. Reverence for the life force and its ever renewing cycles of life and death and life.' There is a clear rhythmic paradigm here with life and death as the primary interconnecting opposites.

Another way in which modern paganism is rhythmic and non hierarchical, connects to its attitude to gender. 'Paganism recognizes the divine, which transcends gender, acknowledging both the female and male aspects of Deity.' (7) The honoring of balance in nature is matched by the balancing of gender in its organizations. For example, in Wiccan covens there is usually a high priestess as well as a high priest. Goddesses are worshipped as much, if not more than gods. Women are often seen as holding greater spiritual power, even where this may be sucked from them and exploited by males. And even though there are still many hierarchies in paganism, powerful leadership positions are often held by women. This can be seen as a

Moon Goddess

move to begin the loosening up of gender inequalities.

Interfaith Rhythms

Paganism can provide a radical kind of interconnection between different faiths. It goes to the simplest of roots of all the religions and is more about nature than about books and dogmas. Frequently, the connections between faiths are made through those at the top of the ladders, as is the case when Christian church leaders meet with Rabbis and Muslim leaders. These are usually male, middle aged and hold a very 'important' rank. Often they are out of touch with the youth on the streets. With hierarchical models on which monotheistic religions have been built, there is a strong sense of 'my religion is better than yours'. 'My religion is the only path to God'. 'My god is the only God.' Groups still sell their path as the best or even only way. And when they meet, their politeness is mixed with hidden power structures. I attended one such meeting under the umbrella of Spirit Matters. There was a table for all the leaders to place their holy books. Unconsciously the Rabbi put his book half on top of the Koran. The Palestinian Mullah pointed this out surprisingly calmly, with a sigh of resignation.

Most people in the world are brought up within one religion or another. And within all of them are roots that involve a connection with nature. Another approach to inter-faith work is tuning into the rhythms of nature together. It involves feeling what we all have in common, not seeing any one religion as better than another. This is the way of rhythm in which the opposites are horizontally related with the possibility of movement and interconnection, without one having to win.

An example of this interconnection was at the Iranian spring festival of Noruz. I was asked to contribute a pagan presence at an inter-faith celebration of the spring Equinox and the Iranian Kurdish new year. It was held in a peace and reconciliation center at St Ethelburga's church, in the city of London, that had been hit by an IRA bomb and rebuilt. The church, like so many in the area, was built over a pre-Roman pagan site, sacred to the goddess of London.

The church was filling up slowly. Kurdish families arrived early to support the musicians, prams were fitted in to the space. Christian couples sat quietly waiting. Iranian students created a buzz at the back. And then at last the Zorastrians arrived. They looked magnificent in glittering robes as they set out the traditional table with its many sacred items. These included a bowl with very fast growing lentil shoots tied with a ribbon. These plants that can almost be seen actually growing, are an ancient symbol of the power of nature at springtime.

In the Mediterranean they were called Gardens of Adonis. He was the lover of the Anatolian goddess Cybele, who dies and was reborn, symbolizing the rhythm of nature itself. The lentil sprouts are a sign of the force of nature's growing power. This image still kept alive at Noruz in Iran and elsewhere, probably goes back to pre-patriarchal time. It is a living picture of the nature god before he became personified.

Prayers were chanted and translated in front of the table. Stories were told of the history of Zorastrianism. Slides were shown of Kurdish Noruz celebration and how they used to be banned in Turkey. Then it was my turn to contribute the pagan part. I shared how whatever religion we are or none we experience the coming of spring and the human meanings we attach to it. Common connections were made with Zorastrians and others, going back thousands of years. Then I told the story of the dying and resurrecting of the goddess Ishtar's consort Tammuz, in Babylon and the weeping of women for him, which is also described in the Bible.

Next, we visualized the fire in the open air, which has always been such a vital part of pagan spring festivals. The fire it also important at Noruz where people jump over it seven times and leave all their sadness behind. So everyone was asked to imagine leaving whatever they wanted to let go of, in the fire. They all had a paper leaf on their chair on which they were asked to write what they wanted to renew for themselves on one side, and overleaf, what they wanted for the planet. These leaves were held in a prayerful pose for a while. Later they were tied on to a tree close by. Afterwards people of the Bha'i faith sang some beautiful prayers to nature. It all ended with some wild and passionate Kurdish circle dancing.

It was all about rhythm. There was the rhythm of the music, the rhythm of nature as a theme, and the rhythmic interplay of the different faiths and none, weaving in and out of each other. Then the rhythmic vibrations of the energy expressed and shared joined all our hearts in an unseen dance of love. Several people came up afterwards to say that they had never met a pagan before, and found the way I had connected every-thing really inspiring. Their fears and prejudices around paganism had changed.

In Islam, Ramadan is attuned to the moon and at the end of the month of fasting the new moon has to be actually visible before the fast can end. Fasting itself is a rhythmic action. It attunes us to the suffering of starving people everywhere. And it also helps our bodies attune to the very natural opposites of feeding and not feeding, of control and consumption, of having and not having, giving and receiving. This is so different from the prevailing Western notion of having more and more, taking in more and more, and endlessly increasing consumption. Daily prayers are also attuned to rhythm of the sun, rising and setting. Other ways of connecting traditional religions with nature's rhythms include winter Solstice celebrations and full moon prayers that are held in churches.

The date of the Christian Easter is still connected to the moon, providing one way that Christians hold on to a long forgotten lunar connectedness. After hundreds of years of neglect, the full and new moons are being noticed more and more in the modern western world. Lovers and poets, farmers and fishermen have always been aware of lunar rhythms, but city life and electricity has lost this connection for millions of others. At last that is changing. Pagan groups meet and do rituals on the full and new moons, in kitchens on high rise estates and in suburban living rooms … as well as naked in the woods! Even urban dwellers are remembering the moon and raves are often held at the time of the full moon.

Goddess Spirituality

Then there is the goddess spirituality movement. The very idea of a goddess rather than a god is a rhythmic thought. It turns the deeply ingrained idea of a male god in the collective unconscious, on its head. It can be seen that this shift is an attempt to equalize the prevailing emphasis on masculine power, and to balance things. We have already seen in the introduction, that some goddess spirituality leaders are thinking of her more as a process in nature than as one or more actual entities. Many mainstream Christian and Judaic leaders will now talk of 'she' as well as 'he' when talking of the divine. And the word 'Allah' has no gender at all, a fact few non-Muslims realize. Goddess spirituality is another way of describing the flow, the equalizing rhythms themselves.

'Goddessing' is a word that symbolizes that the goddess is the process of change, not a being to be worshipped. In the Goddessing' group I used to facilitate we related our personal changes to the external rhythms of sun and moon and the seasons. Winter is often a time for going inside, cutting off from the world and attending to the unconscious psyche. Powerful dreams demanding attention often occur at this time. There can even be depression. Then in the spring there is a renewal of energy and people sometimes feel a sense of inner resolution and want to act out their new found wisdom in the world. Of course not everyone's psychological journey fits neatly into natural rhythms. But contrary to the idea that we should always be happy, sadness, darkness and grief for what has been lost, all have their place in our psychological rhythms. A woman may want to sit in silence all evening. She is in her dark time and we all respect that. The room we met in was painted in the warm red of ancient Cretan temples. It felt like a womb that accepts and transforms all that is brought. Like the souls of the ancients at death 'she' welcomes them all back. And there is a mysterious transformative process that seemed to happen in the sharing, meditation and guided journeys. People generally went away with some resolution to a problem.

I see many people involved in the Pagan movement who want to deepen their practice and clear out the emotional blocks that stop them fully tuning into the rhythms of goddess or nature. For some women, like Susie aged 60, who feel abandoned or neglected by their mothers, the work includes sharing that grief and giving them re-mothering in the therapy. But it can also involve finding goddess images and energies to feel comfort from. She chose the goddess Innana and could actually sense herself being held. She used to softly repeat the name of Innana whenever that abandoned feeling returned.

For other pagans, the goddess can actually be a block. Steve, a man of 50, had projected all his power first onto his mother and then onto 'the goddess', and needed to learn to work with her in a different way. The boy inside him both revered her and was raging with fury. Over time he learnt in therapy to express the fury. He also saw that the hierarchical structures he had built up around him were superficial and unsafe. They were just the surface appearance of manliness and power. The inner boy was playing the game of being a man in an 'important' job and in a 'superior' role to women. Now, through years of inner work he started to empower his real self at a deeper level. He got in touch with the Green god within representing his own natural masculinity. And through this he began to trust his own intuition rather than always taking the lead from women. He can now trust the rhythms of his own body and not just live in the hierarchically thinking head. He can be in charge when it's appropriate and let go more easily when it's not. Now he does not have to always rebel and rage at the goddess either. He can just dance with her.

Women too can have inner hierarchies that stop us dancing our own rhythms. One client called Daisy, 29, had for years unconsciously worshipped her absent father. In spite of being a pagan and loving the goddess, there was the God/father within. She had to learn to see him as the mixture of strong and vulnerable that he really was. By appreciating the opposites in him, she was more and more able to value those in herself. In particular her own inner strength came out. There was a time where she had to identify with the warrior goddess archetype. Daisy internalized the power of Artemis with her arrows, to go straight to the point and become more assertive. Eventually she was able to dance her own rhythms and be strong when she needed to be and vulnerable without fear. What the transformation to rhythmic living creates is a kind of authentic freedom. Through dancing between the opposites within we can dance with others in a more fluid and equalizing way.

Things to do: Getting in Tune with the Moon
1. Keep a moon diary. Notice phases of the moon and what happens in your life to coincide with them. Notice how your emotions and energy levels relate to the moon.

2. Keep a sun dairy. Notice how the seasons affect your moods.

3. Devise your own ritual for some change you desire in your life.

Light candles and burn incense. Visualize and call on whatever god or goddess image represents your need. 'Speak' to them and listen to your intuition replying. Image yourself in the change that you desire, with their presence and support.

4. Think about your own inner opposites. Visualize a mask or costume to represent an opposite side of yourself that you rarely express. Make it. Throw a masked party. Wear it.

5. Find somewhere to dance regularly, even if it's just alone in your kitchen.

CHAPTER FIVE

SPIRITUALITY WITH EQUALITY
AT ITS HEART

Most religions have somewhere in their doctrine, a belief in the equal valuing of all human beings, and indeed of all creation. Yet hierarchical structures and models of thinking are deeply entrenched. There is the obvious ladder to heaven, with God at the top, priests or male religious leaders next, then men, then women then nature at the bottom. Then there's the 'my God is better than your god' hierarchy. But hierarchical thinking underlies much that is written, even in modern spirituality.

New Wine in Old Bottles
One example of old hierarchical thinking in modern spirituality, is in Ken Wilber's influential book *Up from Eden*[1] about the linear evolution of modern human's consciousness from lower to higher states. He admired the perennial philosophy in which 'the great chain of being moves ... from matter to body, to mind, to soul, to spirit'. It goes from 'the lowest rung of the ladder up to the highest – spirit and ultimate wholeness'. Wilber sees more 'primitive' societies as having 'lower' kinds of consciousness, which are sometimes called 'magical'. His hierarchical model rests heavily on the work of the Jungian, Erich Neumann[2] who wrote in the 1930s, 1940s and 1950s when tribal societies were much less respected than today. For these thinkers, it's not just about difference, but about lower and higher rank. On close examination, the vertical structure of Wilber's thought is not just unconscious, unintentional, or even simply a minor detail, it is central. He actually says, 'Rungs on a ladder ... will have to serve as our guiding spatial metaphor.' However he did modify that model in later.

Even modern evolutionists don't see a simple linear progression from bacteria to humans, as if from inferior to superior. Of course, there has been a gradual increase in complexity, but things could have gone in so many other possible directions. It can be seen as a co-creative process that includes so many forces that we still don't understand as well as those we do. Darwin actually said, 'It's not the strongest of the species who survive, nor the most intelligent, but the ones most responsive to change.'

The whole idea of human spiritual evolution from low to high is deeply problematic. To counteract that argument, it has even been argued that humans were better off in every way, including spiritually, when we were hunter-gatherers 20,000 years ago. It is likely that we were probably more able to attune to the spiritual forces around us then. And perhaps that is a more advanced kind of spirituality than in organized patriarchal religion. I would not personally go that far. But it is important to notice wherever hidden, or not so hidden, hierarchical thought patterns come up in someone's ideas.

This sense of a whole range of possible, alternative routes is even more true of human history. Things could have gone in so many different directions. Was the rise and rise of patriarchy inevitable? I often wonder how Western culture might have developed differently if, say, there had not been a volcanic eruption on Thera that helped to destroy the more feminine and egalitarian Minoan civilization.

A client called Jemma, 28, had been a Buddhist for many years. It gave her peace and a philosophy to live by. Her atheist parents had been puzzled at first. They were liberal academics who had rejected the Hinduism of their own backgrounds. They tried to understand. They assumed it was just a rebellious phase she was going through. Jemma argued with them that Buddhism did not require belief in a God of any kind. It was a beautiful philosophy noticing how everything is always changing and showing that there is no point in being attached to anything. But as she became more involved with a particular group, Jemma found herself being judged more and more. There were rigidly defined ways of meditating and the master's word was law. She read articles about the 'backwardness' of Hinduism, associating it with an earlier level of the evolution of consciousness. This was the last straw. Jemma surprised herself by feeling deeply defensive about her almost forgotten ancestral background. An inner conflict began to tear her apart, and she couldn't talk about it to her parents as they would have said, 'I told you so!' So she came to therapy. By talking and doing simple breathing meditation in the sessions she came to separate out the useful parts of Buddhism from the vertical thinking that upset her. She also began to explore the Hinduism that her parents had rejected, and she left her finance job in the Corporate world to teach in an inner city school

Hierarchical models of thinking have been at the root of so many problems in the world, from thousands of years of warfare, racism and sexism to the extreme consumerism that is destroying our planet today. One example of the subtle effect of vertical paradigms appeared in February 2006 on www.integralworld.net – a website connected to Wilber. That month there was a global controversy about the publication of cartoons in Denmark showing the prophet Mohammed with a bomb. Most thoughtful and progressive minded people chose not to publish it. Wisdom can sometimes be more important than truth. However on integralworld.net there was an article by Ray Harris[3] criticizing progressive Westerners for sympathizing with Muslims. He argued that it is because of 'post colonial guilt' which 'ignores the fact that the colonialist stage is part of a developmental spectrum from tribal societies to early state societies, to imperialist power to post imperial power.' He positively quotes Ibn Warraq, who left Islam and writes of 'caving in to societies with a medieval mind set' and urges 'a show of unashamed, noisy solidarity with the Danish cartoonists.' This lack of sensitivity, unawareness of global inequalities and political complexity could have come straight from the pages of a right wing newspaper. It is not what you might expect on an integral philosophy web site.

Then there are the overtly hierarchical attitudes of groups like the

Theosophists who believe in a brotherhood of 'realized disembodied souls' who are leading or even dictating human evolution. Sometimes they are even referred to as 'the hierarchy'. They, like Wilber and many others, argue that the world today badly needs a widespread leap in human spiritual development. But the idea that this leap must be led by an elite, whether from the other dimensions or from a tiny group of 'developed' Americans, does not have to follow.

We are interconnected fluid networks, not rigid pyramid structures. In today's world we all need to learn to trust our very deepest intuition, and the wisdom of the equalizing rhythms that flow throughout the universe. Surely we can still learn from and value highly spiritually developed individuals, without creating new hierarchies. Deep wisdom allows change to unfold without trying to control it. Even modern, non-religious spirituality can seem like new wine in old bottles. The new wine is the flow of transformative energy that the human race so badly needs. But the old bottles are the hierarchical mind sets through which this energy is still being poured.

New Wine in old bottles

Is Spiritual Development Inevitably Hierarchical?

It feels important to distinguish between spiritual development, and a hierarchy in which one group is seen as superior to and ruling over, or in control of others who are seen as inferior. Obviously, some human individuals are more spiritually developed than others, or have special gifts, like shamans, psychics or mystics. In the same way, some people are better musicians or athletes than others. But this does not automatically put them in a position of ruling. They might teach or guide others. But it is usually only where there are traditional religious hierarchies that teachers are expected to literally rule over others. Interestingly, most humans who have been recognized as highly spiritually developed have not chosen to be authoritarian. Indeed they are often admired for their lack of hierarchical attitudes. For example, Jesus befriended prostitutes, which was shocking for his day. Mohammed had a black companion, also shocking for his day. The Buddha left the privileges of his palace to share the suffering of the less fortunate.

There are many spiritual traditions where training comes from being at the feet of a master. This vertical relationship may be seen as necessary for the 'disciple' to surrender their ego and merge with the divine or attain enlightenment. But such paths have usually been part of a society seeped in patriarchal and hierarchical structures. Most progressive people, not only in the West but in the East too, want more equal societies. This has put many off religion all together. But you can still respect and learn from a spiritual teacher without being ruled by them. You may be inspired by their company, but not want to be told what to wear or eat!

A client called Bob, 56, had never known his father. He was the result of an affair his mother had with a married man. All his life there had been this fantasy of some perfect father who would one day come and rescue him. His mother married and had three other children who seemed to be loved more than him. Bob was a sensitive child and started to 'see' spiritual presences around him from the age of six. He trained as a carpenter and loved working with wood, but often felt lonely. In his twenties he discovered Sufism which made sense of his 'visions' and gave him a community to belong to. He quickly became devoted to the Sheikh of that particular order. He was often to be found sitting at his side. But the techniques used to train in this Sufi order include humbling, rejections and humiliation to get rid of the ego. So the Sheikh ignored Bob. After several years, Bob became despairing and suicidal. In therapy his feeling were related to the loss and idealization of his father. But we would also read Sufi scriptures together and honor the valuable essence of the path. Once he had worked through his father issues and developed a sense of self, Bob was able to let this self go. He surrendered to the flow and discovered healing powers that he began to use on others.

While on a spiritual path of any kind it is hard not to see some people as superior to others. They may be better at meditation or more blissed out, or may seem kinder or more peaceful. But none of this makes them an intrinsically superior human being. The division of people into inferior and superior happens in the mind so quickly, it is almost unconscious, and is certainly taken for granted in most modern human cultures. Only at times of deep love and wisdom are most people able to really experience others as truly equal. Many of us can't easily just learn from someone more spiritually developed, without putting them on a pedestal. And then we usually want them to be perfect. When they turn out to be only human and flawed, we can be deeply disappointed and even turn away from the path. This not only comes from our own inner hierarchical structures but also perhaps from the desire for a perfect parent.

Then there is our own spiritual pride. We can create personal inner hierarchies through a feeling of superiority over others. We can even be so passionately against the whole idea of having an adored guru who can do no wrong, that we create yet another unconscious vertical model. There is the superior 'anti' position and the inferior situation of those people who had to have gurus. This is being still stuck in the authoritarian rebel phase described previously. In fact, by taking such a passionate 'anti' stance, we are just as hooked into the hierarchical system as we would be if we were actually sitting at a teacher's feet in India.

I want to suggest that a hidden aim in most spiritual paths is actually to dissolve rigid inner verticalities, and replace them with rhythmic ways of thinking, feeling and living. Every minute of every day can be an opportunity for this transformation.

Dissolving Inner Hierarchies

When we look at the essence of most spiritual paths, within or outside religions, there is the rhythm model, before our very eyes. It flows deep under the edifices of dogma and doctrine. In some traditions like Sufism, it is seen as a river. In native spiritualities, such as African religions, there are also the actual sounds of the beating of the drums. And we have seen the importance of tuning into the rhythms of nature, and observing the phrases of the moon and sun, in practically all spiritualities. But there is one rhythm that stands out with particular immediacy. It is the one rhythm we can be conscious of every minute of every day. It is of course the rhythm of the breath.

1. Rhythms of breathing.

The very word spirit comes from the Latin for breath. Breath is obviously rhythmic. We cannot go on just breathing in for ever. There must be an out breath to balance. For most of us, most of the time it is an automatic rhythm that simply happens naturally. We can practice a whole variety of breathing exercises, which have been important in many traditions. But there is still always the underlying rhythmic form.

The breath also has the quality of being unseen by the naked eye. We know it is there but we can't see it. So it is a powerful metaphor for the unseen world of spirit. And perhaps the movement of spirit in the unseen dimensions also flows rhythmically like the breath. As we have already explored, there does seem to be a balancing process going on in unseen dimensions and rhythm is the form taken by the flow between all kinds of opposites. Feeling breath as wind may also liken it to the experience of many psychics when they are channelling information from the other dimensions. 'It is like a whirring sensation around my head' one psychic told me. I imagine these unseen forces spatially as spiralling swirls of air. This picture could not be more different from the image of a rigid vertical ladder.

If we had no other discipline, this attention to breathing rhythms alone would help us develop. It calms us down when we simply pay attention to it. When I started meditating 40 years ago and was asked just to follow the breath, I could not focus. Then I found that counting with a number on each breath helped me concentrate. Even now I still start my practice with this approach. But everyone has their different methods. In a rhythmic spirituality, techniques are geared to individual needs rather than proscribed for all.

In everyday life, remembering the rhythm of the breath can bring us into the present moment, helping to stop busy minds. Another rhythm we can use involves words to go with the breath. These can be 'mantras' which are often given to initiates by a master, as in the Hindu tradition. But this is a hierarchical system, as the recipient has no choice about their mantra. In a more rhythmic, creative approach to spirituality people can make up their own. To follow the rhythm of the breath it helps if they are of only two syllables. This word can then attune to the in and out breath. 'Here and now', 'thank you' or 'peace full' are some I have used, as well as goddess names such as 'Rhe-aaa'. We can attune this breathing/sound to our needs. When we are tired, a long in breath is helpful. And when we are stressed or panicked, a longer out breath is calming.

Hierarchical thinking is often behind everyday stresses .The mind is so full of little vertical thoughts, dividing the present from the future, good self from bad self. Distractions easily enter the mind: 'I must do this or that, rather than focus on what I'm doing now' or 'I am bad because I did this or that, or didn't do this or that.' Or we become obsessed by the thought that 'this person is bad because they ignored me' or 'the future will be better than now'. To live rhythmically is to notice minute by minute when we are in a vertical thought trap and then transform it to rhythm. For example, we might be feeling fear because of a power inequality such as that with a boss or a super cool friend. Then we can question the hierarchy, tell ourselves that the rhythm of life changes everything, and bring our consciousness straight back to the breath. By focusing on the real, physical, present rhythm of breathing, the thoughts that led to fear often dissolve.

The breathing rhythm can also be used to synchronize with that other everyday rhythm, of walking. If we are able to go really slowly, each step can correspond with one in breath and one out breath. It may not be a good idea to try this in a crowded shopping mall. The two syllable words or mantras we have chosen can be used at the same time as walking. Then there is a concentration on three different rhythms simultaneously. For people with over active minds, this can be a great advantage. The more rhythms being attended to at one time the less space for unhelpful runaway thinking.

2. The equalizing of each moment.

Another way of expressing deep equality is to see the equal value of each moment of time. A minute spent opening a door, chopping vegetables or walking alone is just as valuable as a minute spent writing a book or making love. Can we convince ourselves that this is true? As we go through the day can we simply notice when we are thinking about the future or past as being more important than the present? When we notice, we can just gently come back to the here and now. As Thich Nhat Hann[4] says, 'Every moment is a wonderful moment.' One of the first spiritual books that I read in the 1960s was called *Be Here Now* by Ram Dass[5]. It sounds so easy, but turns out to be just about the most difficult skill in life.

One trick is to stop in the middle of a park, on a train or half way up an escalator and just say 'wow! this is a wonderful moment.' The more unlikely that the particular moment would normally be thought wonderful, the more powerful the technique. When taking out the garbage, it is especially helpful to say, 'This is indeed a magic moment'. In *The Power of Now* Eckhart Tolle[6] shows how spiritually empowering it is to live more fully in the present.

The present moment is where we actually are all the time. It is only our minds that take us off to other times and other places. And to fully focus on what we are actually doing puts us more in touch with the natural rhythms and flows that are happening anyway. For example, eating in a slow conscious way, enables us to feel grateful for every mouthful. And this feeling improves the digestive process with its own automatic balancing of chemicals. It allows our body's rhythms to work without us being in mental control. Being in the present also helps us to attune to the body's rhythm of hunger and satisfaction. When we are full up, we know it, and can stop. Many of us actually go on eating only because we need comfort. Driven by such mental ideas based on an emotional need for something to be different, there is no space for the rhythms to flow naturally. Even our choice of food can come from deep listening to the body's rhythms instead of desperate craving.

In the past, I would often eat for comfort when feeling unhappy or lonely. Food would be stuffed in when I was thinking about something else. I longed for the moment to be different. Being on a retreat where we had silent eating transformed my life. I would take five minutes to eat one grape, looking at it, smelling it. Putting it to my lips, swirling it around, then finally biting into the skin. I would murmur thank you to the universe, so that no one could hear.

Living rhythmically is the opposite of living with addiction, where we want more and more of the same thing. With such attachment to something we haven't got now, or do have, but are afraid of losing, it is not possible to live in the present moment. We are always craving for something in the future. This may not be a substance – it can be a person or even just a pleasurable experience. As William Blake[7] wrote, 'He who binds to himself a joy, does the winged life destroy. He who kisses joy as it flies, lives in eternity's sunrise.' He was talking about living rhythmically.

Consumerism vs Rhythms of Life

As Heraclitus said, 'Everything changes'. It's the one thing we can be certain of. In our present world of speeded up technological and socio-logical change, there is a tendency to cling even more onto things in order to feel safe. Humans evolved physically and psychologically to live in slowly changing societies geared to nature's rhythms. But now we don't easily trust the natural rhythmic changes of life. For example, growing old feels scary, so we try to control it by having plastic surgery or denying the reality. This fear of change in the future stops us living in the present. But it also helps to keep us endlessly consuming products, from the new car with the higher status to the beauty creams to stop wrinkles. The whole of consumer society relies on out dissatisfaction with the present moment and with the rhythms of natural change that go on around us. At the same time we are expected to adapt on an almost monthly basis to new fashion, new technology and even new identities.

We tend to think that we can control our bodies, our minds, our emotions and even our environments by shopping. The truth is that we are destroying the environment not just by buying and using objects like cars, but by buying experiences such as travel to exotic places. 'I shop therefore I am' is the slogan for today. Compulsively shopping is a compensation for our lack of joy in the moment, for being alive and trusting the flow. We have become consumers first and humans second. The whole economic system is geared towards making us buy more and more so that there will be more and more profit and economic growth. The capitalist argument is that this creates more jobs to produce more of all the useless things we end up throwing away. But is this how humans want to live?

There is mounting evidence that after a certain standard of living is reached, in which people are not struggling just to make ends meet, more money does not create more happiness. A quote from the New Economic Foundation states that 'The irony is, that a large body of evidence shows that increased consumption, beyond a level that the UK passed long ago, does nothing to increase our level of well being.' (The UK Interdependence Report, April 2006.)[8] So we are destroying the environment without it even making us happier. But we think consuming makes us happier because of the hierarchies in our heads. Things provide status. Children must have what the other kids have to feel good enough, to be accepted or even to be better than others.

A belief in deep equality, and the value of each individual for themselves, would stop the madness tomorrow. But it would also slow down the economy. The corporations that rule our world today spend millions in advertising to ensure that such an attitude never takes hold. They are even using the language of spirituality these days to sell objects like mobile phones. 'Be in the present and buy this phone.' In reality, mobile phones take people away from the present moment. When talking to someone on a mobile phone it is not likely that we will also notice the spring blossom or even, tragically, an oncoming car. Pedestrian accidents, especially of teenagers using mobile phones are on the increase.

Shopping itself has become the new religion. And it's all about hierarchy. We may have got rid of the old attitudes towards royalty and aristocracy, but they been replaced by celebrities wearing £1,000 earrings. Now everyone is told that they can be like celebrities, if they just buy a cheaper version of the same thing. It is a false kind of equality. The so-called equality of choice, appears to be non-hierarchical, but it relies on people being dissatisfied in the first place. It relies on them craving higher status. It relies on them looking up to or down on others. And the economic reality is that the gap between rich and poor is increasing all over the world. Equality of the theoretical opportunity to buy, is the kind of equality sold to us today. How have we let them fool us so success-fully?

Deep equality is vital for an alternative to the consumer culture that is directly responsible for global warming. Even if governments were to limit our energy use more effectively, deeper changes in the human psyche are clearly also needed. Consuming so much has to be seen as seriously uncool.

A client called Pat, 32, was an accountant in an international financial services firm. Her father's business had failed when she was 11. Both parents had pushed their only child to succeed through school and college. She never questioned the ladder she was on. It was all simply one rung after another, up, up and up. Pat had all the trimmings of success, the good car, the beautiful apartment and designer clothes. Most of her friends were similar. They played hard too, going to the theatre, eating out, having affairs or more often, simply flings. None of them were in or seriously looking to be in long term relationships. They were having too much fun. Yet nothing was ever enough. She wanted a bigger apartment, the latest designer shoes, yet more exotic holidays. There was always the desire for more. Then one woman in the group of friends died suddenly in a car accident. Pat was devastated. Long buried feelings resurfaced. She raged and cried as much for herself as her friend.

In therapy Pat realized that underneath the gloss, there was a deeply hidden sense of failure. Basically she was not good enough. We soon worked out that she was carrying her father's feelings of failure. But we also began to address the loneliness she had been escaping from for years. We built up a strong relationship, where Pat could be herself, with no judgment. Eventually we also explored the third underlying problem, which was a sense of meaninglessness. She had always loved nature so it was natural for her to look at paganism as a spirituality that suited her. Pat joined a coven in New York and began working freelance. She started a serious relationship with another pagan who was a struggling artist, and very different from her other more materialistic friends. At first she kept him a secret. But after six months she finally introduced him to her friends. Sadly, they were as just critical as she feared they would be. But by this time her deep self-esteem had grown enough for her to withstand their comments and carve her own path through the concrete jungle.

Rhythmic Flow as Connectedness
Many spiritual writers talk of the need for us to develop a deeper sense of our interconnectedness. For example, throughout modern spirituality there is the concept of the oneness that connects us all to each other and to everything that is. This is not just an idealistic dream. Many people

have a direct experience of this, as an actual bodily feeling, when in meditation, or in the presence of a teacher, or even just out of the blue on a Monday morning. As Ken Wilber and others show, this feeling happens more frequently as one moves more deeply into a spiritual path. But for most of us, most of the time, there is a big gap between our normal 'dualistic' way of living and the wonderful loss of self in the oneness of it all. So how do we get from one to the other on an everyday basis? I suggest that rhythmic thinking and living is a vital stage in between duality and oneness.

This oneness is usually simply contrasted with being in duality. This is itself a dualistic split way of looking at things. What exactly do we mean by duality? Most of the time our thinking is in opposites and we feel separate. There is me and the others, me and nature or me and the things I do. There is also duality in our thinking. As Jacques Derrida[9] pointed out, we tend to think in binaries or opposites: good and bad, right and wrong, life and death, sun and moon, masculine and feminine. But the problem with dualism or the opposites, is that one is seen as being better than the other. It is not usually about equal opposites dancing in interconnection. The problematic spatial image is vertical not horizontal, rigid rather than rhythmically moving, hierarchical rather than equal.

If we start with where we are, in duality, the question is, 'how can we consciously move towards the oneness?' First it seems that we need to loosen up the dualities, turn the hierarchies upside down. In other chapters we have already seen this done in our everyday life, in small ways, or on a bigger stage at carnival.

If we can open our minds to the rhythm model of thinking about other people, it is a step on the way to oneness. I have had the experience of feeling this great oneness in meditation, but then going to the kitchen to make tea and the hierarchies return. I would ignore the unattractive man in the corner, in order to impress the handsome one at the sink. In the state of oneness itself, I would naturally see no distinctions. It's when I come out of that experience that the problem begins.

When we are in that state of oneness, it is easy for us to glide through each moment feeling as though we are being 'guided' by the divine. We are in the flow, attuning easily to those invisible movements of energy between opposite states. We may not know consciously which opposites are involved. They might be in other dimensions, or in the collective unconscious. For example, at the level of the world soul (anima mundi), there are opposites and balancing processes, just as there are in the individual psyche. One pair could be between the opposites of materialism and spirituality. At present the world soul is experiencing a painful imbalance. Global capitalism, aided by the Enlightenment project, has helped create a deeply materialistic world. The spiritual side has been pushed to an inferior position. And now there is beginning to be an equalizing swing back to putting spirituality higher on the agenda. Unfortunately, this sometimes takes the form of fundamentalist religious fervor and a corresponding loss of other equalities, such as gender. But on the world soul level, the need to balance spirituality with materialism may be the only way we will survive on this planet. So I am suggesting that there is a flow of energy away from materialism towards spirituality. Attuning to this particular flow means giving more personal attention to the spiritual and minimizing the material. Even if it is just meditating or doing yoga every day and giving up the quest for a newer model car, you are following where the deep equalizing energy needs to go.

On an everyday level, there is the sense of flow when we are absorbed in an activity and not using hierarchical thought patterns. But that activity could be against the flow that is needed in the wider world. So it is not just about absorption. We are fully in the flow when things feel intuitively right, harmonious and appropriate in many dimensions. And usually we cannot be logically conscious of all these factors. So our deepest intuition is vital here. And learning to distinguish our deepest intuition from our fears or our desires is a lifetime's work. But we can know when it is working because we find that our flowing activities interconnect with others in what are often called synchronicities. We often feel lighter, less burdened by thoughts and worries. Because timing is such a crucial feature of these meetings or connections, it seems likely that flows happen between time/space opposites that we have no scientific understanding of yet.

One of the most beautiful descriptions of 'the flow' comes from Taoism. Lao Tsu in the *Tao Te Ching* describes the Tao as 'Something mysteriously formed. Born before heaven and earth, In the silence and the void, Standing alone and unchanging, ever present and in motion. Perhaps it is the mother of ten thousand things. I do not know its name. call it Tao. For lack of a better word, I call it great. Being great, it flows. It flows far away, having gone far, it returns.'

'Man follows the earth. Earth follows heaven. Heaven follows the Tao. Tao follows what is natural.'

Many traditions have spoken of surrendering to the flow. This requires enormous trust and openness of heart and a degree of humility that is rare in the modern world. The Sufis are particularly known for their wisdom around surrender and a sense of the divine manifesting in rhythmic, swirling, flowing forms. In order to attune we must become nothing. We must lose control. We must trust. Rumi[10] writes, 'One breath from you and we are unfurled, for a fleeting moment on your dancing breath.' Such letting go requires a deep dissolution of our normal hierarchies of fear, self importance and perfectionism.

Perfectionism and Letting Go

While many of the old hierarchies that kept everyone in place socially, have now gone, new ones have plunged deep into our psyches. Now we are told by the capitalist culture that it is all up to us, by our own efforts we must try to become perfect. Even in the spiritual world there is the idea that we should all strive to achieve a goal. We must get better, better at meditating, better at being good, better at being successful in the world, better at being healthy and fit. Many young people, especially girls, are pushing themselves to have perfect bodies as well as perfect achievement at school and work. This can lead to anorexia and many other physical problems. It is the opposite of trusting the rhythms of nature, trusting one's deepest intuition and trusting the wisdom that comes with living in the present moment.

Even using terms like the 'higher self', which is often used today, gives us a problematic message. It can sound like something superior inside us that should be in control. This way of thinking seems far away from that surrender to the flow that the Sufis talk about. We could say these are just words. Does it matter what we call it? But we have already seen with Wilber that spatial structures behind ideas do matter.

In spite of all my personal attempts to question unconscious hierarchies in my own thinking, I still find myself talking about 'the higher self' a lot. It certainly has been a useful concept for spiritual people who don't want to use the word god or goddess. It took a while for me to find another word. Now, I sometimes use the word 'deepest intuition'. Turning 'higher' into 'deeper' can be a first step in loosening up the whole vertical spatial concept. My sense is that the divine, the flows, the forces affecting us from other dimensions are neither up nor down, from above or below, or indeed vertically organized at all. But as humans we may never be capable of getting our heads round the complex time/space patterns that surround and interpenetrate us.

As we know so little, does not it make sense to trust more and listen more, to empty our minds and to be open. As Rumi wrote, 'Make the moment infinite, beyond the curling snake of passing time and space. Learn to die in the infinitely elusive moment.' It is a death to the ego and to the need for control. As Bhai Sahib said, quoted in Chasm of Fire, Irina Tweedie[11] 'Saints are like rivers. They flow where they are directed ... The river does not know if it is flowing.' Few of us can reach such profound trusting and fluid states. But we can all work at flowing a little bit more, and controlling a little bit less.

Hierarchies of control tend to develop where there is no trust in the flow. They are a kind of compensation. Even praying to an all-powerful superior God to control things for us, is still stuck in the old paradigm. Attuning to God as the divine flow takes a different mind set. It is listening, trusting, surrendering and letting the flow simply flow. Words of pleading or even worship can drown out the sounds of those whispers from the deep. Another way of putting it is to silence the mind completely. We tend to think the idea of trusting in the unseen is reactionary and must lead to fundamentalism and tyranny. But what if in this case the unseen was actually a flow trying to balance out inequalities? What if we allowed ourselves to trust in a deeper equalizing process? What if we are being more truly revolutionary by trusting the flow, than by believing everything has to be consciously controlled by us?

'The highest good is like water.
Water gives life to the ten thousand things and does not strive.
It flows in places men reject and so is like the Tao.' *Tao Te Ching*

In most traditions there is an acknowledgement of the still, empty place from which to 'watch' the flowing of all around. Paradoxically it is when we are in that quiet place that we are most likely to be open to the flow. Or rather, the wise and balancing forces that are appropriate to whatever we are doing, will happen around and though us, when we are still at our center.

'The space between heaven and earth is like a bellows.
The shape changes, but not the form;
The more it moves, the more it yields.
More words count less.
Hold fast to the centre.'
Tao Te Ching

The Mysteries of Rhea / Cybele

The flow has been most clearly personified in the ancient Cretan goddess

Rhea and her Rhythms

Rhea. It is to her mystery cults that we now turn to explore a post-modern way of losing our egos in attunement to the flow. In the 20th Century, Westerners tended to look to the East for deep spiritual wisdom. Yet there have been similar paths to the Sufi, Buddhist or Hindu ones of today, in the past, in the West too. These were almost completely lost under the influence of Christianity. Most of these ancient paths seem to have developed out of the mists of pre-history. We don't even have written information about spiritualities before around 3500 BC in Sumer and 1000 BC in Europe. Even after that time, many libraries, like the one at Alexandria were burned and valuable insights were lost to humanity for ever. But in 'mystery cults' of classical Greece and Rome we can catch a glimpse of what those ancient paths might have included. Much has been written down about them in the historical period from 500 BC to 400 AD.

It seems that many of the mystery 'cults' of the classical world involved stages of spiritual development culminating in a ritual death. This is likely to have been similar to the Sufi approach of dying to the ego in order to surrender to the flow. One of the most respected of these cults was based in Crete and involved the goddess Rhea. She is not particularly well known in the modern neo-pagan world but in the past she represented the mysterious, unspeakable order with nature. She was the divine energy that ancient mystics tuned into. Rhea could be seen as the rhythms of life beneath everything that is. She is the closest goddess in literature to the idea of rhythm and flow. Rhea is often associated with Kybele of ancient Anatolia, who also goes back a long way. Her mysteries on Mount

Ida in Crete were some of most secret and respected of the ancient world. But they were only written about in the Classical period. According to Xenophanes of Colophon,[12] Pythagoras was initiated into the mysteries of Rhea around 500 BC. In those times, science and mysticism were not yet divided.

I first discovered Rhea when on holiday in Crete, one gentle spring in the 1980s. I was with my eight-year-old daughter, who was easily bored. We rushed around the main sites and museums on coach trips for tourists, which was hardly the best way of visiting a place that was to change my life. I was teaching a social anthropology course at the time, and just beginning to explore ancient goddess cultures. Little did I know what a big change was about to happen. Arriving at the site of Knossos, I almost fainted with a powerful sense of having been here before. It was a vast temple site reached by walking up wide and worn down steps from the sea behind. Dark, brooding cypress trees and the clicking of cicadas accompanied our ascent. At the entrance stood a pair of massive reconstructed bulls' horns and to the left were the twin peaks of its protective mountain. It too looked like bulls' horns. And in the frescoes inside were more horns. Everywhere I looked they challenged and excited me. I felt the pull of some primal masculine sexuality. Inside the reconstructed labyrinth with its warm red ochre pillars, I felt completely at home. But most impressive of all was the art. Their murals, painted in soft blues and greens, browns and earthy reds, showing bare breasted women and sensual men, plants and animals, was so flowing, rhythmic and life affirming. The still lines seemed to actually move as you looked. They exuded joy and freedom and a sense of attunement to nature. I also liked the feeling of women being equal. Female figures tended to dominate ritual scenes and were ever present in dignified poses, dancing and even leaping over bulls.

In my research I discovered that although early Cretan writing has not yet been deciphered, later Greek myths describe Rhea as the mother of Zeus, living on Crete. I could feel in my bones that she was the closest we would get to the Cretan name for the divine flow of life that is behind everything. And she was there in all the art, from 3000 BC or before until 1400 BC when the patriarchal Mycenaeans appear to have finally taken over. From then on, the art changes to become much more rigid and geometric.[13]

Out of what we do know from Pythagoreans, I have developed a seven stage initiation process into the mysteries of Rhea / Cybele for post-modern seekers. The immediate intention is to increase our ability to tune in to the flow of the rhythms of life. But the ultimate aim is to increase balancing processes on all levels of life, including the economic and social. By working on the opposites within us, we can affect those dualities that have become so imbalanced in the world soul. It can also be seen as a training in developing and trusting one's deepest intuition. This training is not secret and is certainly not meant to make anyone feel superior to anyone else, because they are 'initiated'. It does not make us 'higher'. It just helps us to be more empty of ego and to 'lead without dominating' as described Tao Te Ching. So this path actually trains us in a different kind of leadership.

Things to do: A Training in the Mysteries of the Flow
These exercises can be done alone or with others, in a day workshop or over a lifetime.

1. **Emptying**: Like in the mysteries of old, it starts with a kind of purification process. As we are getting away from the dualistic hierarchy between pure and impure, we will look at it as letting go, washing away what is not needed for the journey. It involves preparing physically by washing, mentally by emptying thoughts and emotionally by letting go of attachments. This phase can take years of therapy, a lifetime of meditation practice or a single night. The aim is to reach a point where we are able to control the mind enough to empty it completely for at least short periods of time.

Exercise: Practice remembering the rhythm of breath with words to keep you focused all through the day. Use the name of Rhea, Era or any two syllable words that helps. See how long you can stay focused. How far can you walk along a street before the mind takes over?

2. **Trusting**: Then there is the moving to a sacred space, apart from the rest of the world. This requires trust and the ritual aspect of this stage includes being blindfolded and allowing someone to lead the initiate. Going to a sacred cave may not be practically possible. At this stage there needs to be a surrender to the process. The opposites involved in this approach can be represented by black and white clothes. At this point black may be worm and there is a going into the deepest darkness.

Exercise: Find a quiet space to sit down and close your eyes. Imagine that you are in a cave, sitting on a black cushion. It is completely dark. You have no sense of directions or of time. Let the darkness enfold you and let go of any thoughts. Let go of your identity. Become nothing.

3. **Facing fears**: Spending time alone, meditating, allowing fears to come up and be faced is the next stage. The fears may come up as thoughts or images. These can be terrifying, and the task is to stay centered throughout their appearance. Sometimes they may appear as actual visions. They can be worked with in a psychotherapeutic way or simply be allowed to come and go. Staying in touch with ones center is vital here. Loud noises such as the beating of drums, screams and growls may be used at this point.

Exercise: Sit down and close your eyes. Imagine the things you are most afraid of. Picture them vividly. Be aware of the centeredness of your own body, and the imaginary nature of the fears. Wipe them out with an imaginary brush. Recreate them and wipe them out again. Write them down on paper. Burn the paper. Draw or paint them, and look at them till they no longer hold the fear.

4. **Gathering the opposites**: This stage involves an exploration of the opposites within, particularly the shadow sides. Then there is a time to actually act out (safely) one or more sides of the self that are the opposite to the usual way a person is in the world. This may be done out in the

world or within the enclosed sacred space. Dressing up can be an important part of this phase.

Exercise: Take a sheet of paper and draw a line down the middle. Write on one side what characteristics you think most identify you as a person. Then on the other side write the opposite to each one of them. Try for one hour or for a whole day being one of those opposites. Dress up as that opposite. Work your way down the list.

5. **Interconnection of opposites**: (known as Sacred Marriage in some traditions). This involves a bringing together of the opposites in a rhythmic connection, through acting, painting, dancing or in some cases actual love making. There is a deep and full acceptance of the other within the self. Out of this interpenetration of opposites comes a release of love energy. This energy is then dedicated to the dissolving of hierarchies everywhere and the connectedness with the 'other' inside and outside ourselves.

Exercise: Devise a ceremony for you to 'marry' your own opposites within. Have a chair or another person represent the opposite. Then go and be them. Visualize or even enact a sacred marriage in a beautiful, magical setting.

6. **Love under will**: This stage involves the practice of sending love to whoever one chooses. Starting with someone you are or were in love with, and moving on to similar others, and then to people with whom you might have difficulties. This can be done by bringing images of people to mind. Then the heart can be opened as if it were two little doors, and loving energy can be visualized. Words can be spoken under the breath, like 'I love you'. This exercise is very important to carry out in relation to oneself. It can be done in front of the mirror.

Exercise: Every morning look in the mirror and tell yourself how much you love you. Make time each day to do the sending love exercise described above. Use it every time you have difficulties with someone. Remember as you go through the day to be grateful to life, to love what you do, to see beauty in everything.

7. **Commitment to living rhythmically**: In the final stage of initiation there is a change of clothes to show that a transformation has taken place. There is a symbolic surrender to the divine flow. Promises are made to keep practicing the techniques such as breathing, to continue to empty the mind and attune to deep wisdom of the intuition. Each individual makes a plan for their own future development and discipline.

Exercise: Write down on paper a commitment to living rhythmically and to practice the techniques. Devise a ceremony alone or with others to offer yourself to the flow of life, to the wisdom of your own deepest intuition.

CHAPTER SIX

COSMIC RHYTHMS

We are in deep trouble as a planet, and even more as the human race presently inhabiting it. The earth will survive, but can we? The shifts needed, in lifestyles, in attitudes to nature and to each other, as well as in our very deepest structures of thinking, can seem just too enormous.

Capitalism and consumerism feel so entrenched that it is hard to even imagine other ways of living. But consumerism is intimately connected with vertical models of relating, the need for status and so on. Begin to transform hierarchical thinking and other life style changes become easier. Without the prime motivation of competition to be 'higher' than the next person, why would we need that faster car? Most of the things we buy, after we have satisfied our basic needs, are to do with fitting into social hierarchies. We want to keep up with others, be superior to others or to stop feeling inferior to others. Today we have the advertising culture to add pressure to this process. We are urged to shop, shop, shop, till we drop. But most climate change experts agree that we can't go on for many more centuries with this extreme level of consumerism.

Some scientists such as James Lovelock[1] argue that it is already too late. Global warming has gone too far to be reversed. Oil production is thought to be reaching a peak before declining drastically. Irresponsible attitudes toward war, the arms trade and nuclear proliferation have made widespread destruction practically inevitable. If this is the case, our old ways of living and thinking will be impossible anyway. We may be forced to change through no choice of our own. The present era may seem like a distant dream to our great-grandchildren. They will see us as simply partying on the Titanic as it drives full speed ahead towards the hidden iceberg.

So even if we can't change our thinking quickly enough to prevent global catastrophe, perhaps at least we can change it to help us survive into a very different future. The transformation from hierarchical to equalizing rhythmic thinking may be needed for us to remain sane in this new world. We will no longer be able to think in terms of more and more profit, more and more things, higher and higher status. We will have to recycle, to live sustainably, to share and live simply to survive. We will need a different kind of shared spirituality focused on attunement to the rhythms of nature and based on our similarities rather than on hierarchical differences.

Hierarchies Between Humans and Nature
One of the most prevalent hierarchies in our thinking is between humans and nature. The very idea that we are separate from nature would make little sense to our pre-historic ancestors or indeed to tribal peoples today. We are made of the same chemical elements as all of nature. The same rhythms of life operate throughout nature. The same basic principles of eco-systems remaining sustainable affect us too. We may be more complex than our closest relatives in the animal world, but it is only in our structures of thinking that we imagine ourselves to be fundamentally superior to them, or to a tree, for that matter. When we are in the flow, attuning to nature, issues of superior/inferior simply don't enter our heads. This sense of interconnectedness with nature's rhythms is vital for our psychological well being. Many clients refer to the healing power of nature.

Hilary grew up on a farm in the American mid-West. Life revolved around the changes of the seasons and the rhythms of day and night and the birth and death of animals and people. When she started her first period Hilary noticed that it always began at the dark of the moon. She was fascinated by the changes of the moon and her body's relation to them. Hilary was also extremely bright and ended up going to Harvard Law school in the 1990s. She was soon snapped up by one of the top corporate law firms, and moved to New York. To prove she was not just the little farm girl from Ohio, she worked longer and longer hours. By the time she was 37 her periods had become so heavy and painful that she could hardly move. Yet she would drag herself to work regardless of her body 'shouting' that something was wrong. In the winters she became depressed, longing to rest and even stay in bed for days. But there was never the time. She ate on the run, foods that were not in season, without having time to digest them properly. There wasn't even time for 'proper' relationships. Along with most of her colleagues in their thirties, she was having casual sex at conferences.

When she came for therapy Hilary was unconsciously holding her breath. She couldn't even allow the natural rhythm of breathing to flow naturally. The work was about coming back to herself and to the natural rhythms she had forgotten. Simply sitting together and breathing was a start. Then there was the acceptance and valuing of herself as a person and as a woman. Masculine ways were so much more valued in the world she inhabited. Hilary despised women who left the corporate world to become stay-at-home mothers. She also despised her body and tried to control it by jogging and going to the gym early every morning. She was exhausted and it was not until she forced herself to rest that Hilary began to open to deeper change.

A vivid dream of a large black woman in flowing blue robes on a boat, led her to explore goddess spirituality. She joined a coven in New York and began honoring the changing of the seasons and the rhythms of the moon. She created huge female sculptures that helped eventually to heal her womb that had been in so much pain. A few years later she left the corporate job and joined a women's community in up state New York where she could be creative and attune more effectively to nature's rhythms.

This belief in our separateness from nature and our superiority over nature, has become deeply ingrained in most cultures of the world. At least since the days of Plato, most Western thinking and much Eastern philosophy has been shaped by a ladder structure. In this hierarchy, pure ideal abstract forms are at the top and material nature is at the bottom. Our physical body is seen as material substances, while our minds are 'higher'. Humans are not only thought of as superior to nature, but we are meant to control it too. The hierarchical, ladder model generally leads to dominating behavior, as action tends to follow thought. This way of thinking creates a strong sense that our 'inferior' bodies being 'closer to nature', are supposed to be controlled by our 'superior' minds. In such a world, there is no room for listening to the wisdom of the body, or even for learning from nature. Yet nature has so much to teach us, if we listen wisely. Listening wisely is very different from projecting our own human ideas onto her. Some writers have pointed to the enormous amount of co-operation in nature, as in beehives, to argue that co-operation is even more a part of nature than competition. Others just see hierarchies. Nature can be used to argue for any kind of human arrangement. But what works for bees does not necessarily work for humans.

Rhythm at the Heart of Nature
Instead of transposing animal or insect social organization from nature to humans, we could look at the underlying deep structures of nature to learn from. What are these deep structures? Are they the very rhythmic forms that we have been exploring in these pages? To explore these forms further, we need to enter the realms of physics and mathematics, quantum and string theories as well as ecology and biology. We need to travel into the heart of nature with our imagination as well as with our reason. There in the very deepest structures of nature we discover an order that can give us a more basic alternative to hierarchy as a central organizing principle. That order can be described as deep equality, an endless rhythmic equalizing process occurring at many levels. To explore this we are not only looking through microscopes or telescopes at bits of nature, but looking through time itself at patterns. Using intuition as well as science, experience as well as theory, imagination as well as reason, we find endless balancing, oscillating rhythmic processes. If we think of

Yin and Yang in Multidimensional Zones

balancing as being a form of equalizing, we have a basic principle of nature, a kind of very simple order. It is the order of rhythm, in which high becomes low and back again. Dark becomes light and back again. This simple principle can provide a powerful metaphor for better human living. In fact it has already been the foundation of ordinary wisdom for thousands of years. 'What goes up must come down. What you give out is what you get back.' These are all common sayings in most cultures.

This order can be seen as a metaphor for the human need to equalize that we explored in earlier chapters. The general principle of equalizing rhythm can occur on many levels and in many dimensions. Each zone has its own particular science, from biology to cosmology, from physics to psychology. These different sciences provide evidence on their separate levels. But it can be said that, in a sense, everything is moving between opposites, maybe very fast, or very slowly. All life is rhythm. Everything is vibrating in different frequencies. The manifestation in nature of this rhythmic principle can be described by science but it would not of course be seen as itself a scientific principle. It is too general.

Scientists can measure the many equalizing rhythms, like light waves or brain rhythms. They can show that rhythms from different levels can synchronize with each other. For example, it is well known that tidal rhythms of the sea connect with moon rhythms. What is less well known in our post agricultural era, is that many animals and plants also synchronize with the moon. Hundreds of other rhythmic relationships are described by Lyall Watson in *Supernature*.[2]

Science can also demonstrate the importance of self-regulation in nature. This is itself a rhythmic principle, when one extreme is reached there is natural flow back to the opposite. This comes from a kind of homeostasis in which chemicals are endlessly balancing themselves. For example, when in nature, there is too much oxygen, levels are automatically reduced. Lovelock writes about this in relation to the whole planet and the atmosphere around it. His poetic use of the name Gaia for the earth has inspired millions. She is seen as a live self-regulating body. He describes this homeostatic rhythm as 'an endless balancing movement of energy between extremes'.

This book is of course, not a formal scientific treatise, using evidence and proof. It is an exploration of ideas linking rhythms of nature to social and psychological changes needed to be addressed by humans. There are many scientists who refer to the rhythmic and non-hierarchical principles that underlie nature and apply to human society. The biologist Elizabeth Sahtouris has related patterns in nature to what is needed in society at this time of crisis. She uses the metaphor of dance and the endless creativity and balancing that goes on in nature. She also stresses that any model we make of nature is at heart metaphorical. Such metaphors are vital pointers to ways for us humans to learn to think and live differently. She argues that it is 'Gaian wisdom to balance variety and use it creatively in forming a stable eco-system ... and trends towards more Gaian networks in place of top-down authoritarian structures are emerging in new organizations ... as they decentralize their management and make it more concentric than hierarchical.' [3]

A management consultant was working for a firm producing health foods. The company was started by a very charismatic woman, who started the business from her own kitchen. As it got bigger and bigger and employed more and more people, the organization became more hierarchical. Yet the ethos of the project was all about sustainability and egalitarianism. When the contradictions became too uncomfortable and some employers started going off sick, the consultant was brought in. She interviewed everyone individually and gave them all the same amount of time, regardless of where they were in the hierarchy. During meetings she even equalized by giving more attention to the shy but perceptive older woman than to the two confident young men at the front. The main opposites that had become vertically divided were responsibility and irresponsibility. Middle management had become over responsible, unable to delegate and working long hours. Employees at the 'bottom' had become increasingly irresponsible as they were given less and less power over their work.

The middle managers were encouraged to take less responsibility and be more willing to delegate. In that way everyone could partake in a natural rhythm of being appropriately responsible sometimes and letting it go at other times. The rhythmic approach was developed in other ways to fit in with seasonal business, and weekly group meetings were established for feedback. There was a flow of information in two directions from the top down and from the bottom up. This set up a natural self-regulation process to do with the needs of the tasks, not to do with power for power's sake. But eventually the whole structure had to change and everyone was given power over projects appropriate to their abilities and interests as well as more similar pay.

Rhythm in String Theory

Another way of looking at rhythms in nature comes from a relatively new scientific theory. String theory was developed through attempts to bring Quantum Theory together with the Theory of General Relativity. While one looked at the unpredictable behavior of smaller and smaller sub atomic particles, the other looked at the larger forces of gravity, time, energy and matter. While reminding ourselves that cosmologists still only understand five per cent of the universe (the other 95 per cent is unknown 'dark matter/energy'), these large forces do all seem to involve tension between opposites. For example, electromagnetic energies come from the tension between negative and positive. This is even the case at the atomic level between the 'positive' proton and the 'negative' electron. Even gravity needs two bodies. Somehow the dance between opposites seems an essential feature of the universe in one way or another. In String theory this 'dance' becomes a fundamental property of the tiniest 'bits' yet imagined. The hypothesis is that everything is basically made up of oscillating 'strings'. They are supposed to be like minute loops or elastic bands 'twanging' in different ways for different sub atomic particles. One kind of 'twang' creates electrons and another kind of 'twang' creates neutrons, another particular oscillation creates protons, and yet another lower vibration may create gravitons (particles of gravity). All these subatomic particles are actually vibrating strings rather than single points.

String theory is still just a theory, worked out mathematically without, as yet, concrete evidence, although scientists are working on proof at vast underground tunnels at the famous CERN laboratory on the French/Swiss border. But in order for the hypothesis to work there must be at least nine spatial dimensions, instead of our familiar three. Time is sometimes called the 4th dimension. The other six spacial dimensions appear to be kind of curled up. Some scientists have even wondered whether there are more time dimensions. Perhaps those too are curled up! A psychic once told me through a 'channelled message' that time is like a pipe cleaner, with two or more lengths of string wound around a flexible stick, then each one of them curled around the other! The geometry of these dimensions is hard for us to get our heads around. The idea of pipes with 'strings' curled around inside is often used. And these pipes can go round in circles themselves, leaving a hole in the middle. Doughnut shapes have been suggested as useful images. There is also the Calabi-Yau space, which tries to visualize the extra spatial dimensions of string theory curled in and through each other.

And then there is the concept of spin. Strings can be seen as spinning through space. As Brian Greene[4] put it, 'being in a winding mode is a possibility inherent to strings'. This winding, spinning, wriggling motion is also the way that mystics, shamans and psychics have described the universe for thousands of years. Sometimes, as Jeremy Narby[5] demonstrates, this perception literally involves 'seeing' the image of entwining serpents dancing through the cosmos. Rainbow serpents moving through the cosmos are also described by Australian Aborigines.

Scientific understanding of these extra dimensions and the primacy of vibration and spin may one day help explain a whole range of mysterious human experiences in altered states of consciousness. People seeing the future could be tuning in to curled up time or spinning seventh dimensional space.

At the present time, proponents of String Theory such as Brian Green and Edward Whitten[6] show that it is the most elegant, most likely, 'theory of everything'. As Brian Green writes, 'If string theory is right, the microscopic fabric of our universe is a richly entwined multidimensional labyrinth within which the strings of the universe endlessly twist and vibrate, rhythmically beating out the laws of the cosmos.' The same oscillating and spinning forms may be forever emerging on vastly different scales. The basic patterns may be the same whether at the sub atomic or cosmic levels. At least we can say that the images evoked by this new science are of oscillating rhythms and spinning spirals, curling through space and time. These models of thinking are very different from the more mechanical notions of straightforward Newtonian cause and effect. Frijof Capra[7] has written at length about this difference between the old mechanical world view and the new one of interconnected systems with rhythms at their heart.

So How Do We Attune to These Unseen Rhythms?

Attuning to rhythms, from the very small and fast to the very big and slow, seems to be implicit in many forms of spiritual practice. Meditation changes the speed of brain rhythms. Breathing slowly changes yet another rhythm in order to calm the mind. But what about the unseen 'strings' oscillating in and between unseen dimensions. Can we also

Winding out of the Seventh Dimension

attune to these? Is being in the flow actually about this kind of multidi-mensional attunement? Are our internal 'strings' vibrating at the same frequencies as external 'strings'? Is this easier to do when we empty our minds and let intuition take over? Sometimes we need a dramatic push to move into this deep attunement. In ancient times initiation rites helped this process. Today we can use different forms of initiation. This is sometimes provided through intense relationships.

Three years ago I met a beautiful young man who seemed to me like a messenger from the other dimensions. He was to lead me through an extraordinary series of 'initiations' to become one with the flow. The first night I went to his flat, he appeared different, strange, wild and unshaven, which was unusual for him. I thought I had made a terrible mistake, and my body literally shook in terror for two hours, apparently releasing the fears of many lifetimes. Then I suddenly had the thought that all he needed was my love. Instantly the fear vanished. I surrendered to whatever was in store and was no longer in control. Weeks later we were sitting in deep meditation facing each other and holding hands. I saw his face transform into a hundred different masks, from skulls to pirates. My face changed for him too. We just stayed staring at each other for what seemed like hundreds of years, but was actually just one night.

During our time together my 'guide' had several dreams associating me with rivers. One was specifically about the Thames. Another was of me beside a more ethereal silver river, looking peaceful and radiating love, unlike my normal anxious self! He had turned me into his teacher just as he was my teacher. For a few weeks I even became this being, and experienced powerful currents of love pouring through me. Then another event took place while we were making love on May Day. I was lying down and he was sitting up barely touching me. At first it was just ordinary and extraordinary sexual bliss. Then for the first time in my life I experienced actually becoming a river. It wasn't coming through me, or out of me, I was it. The river seemed to be the Nile, which was strange as I don't have much connection with Egypt. He was a perfectly formed, perfectly still stone statue. My whole body was streaming for what felt like hours. I was one with the river and had no separate identity. After this 'initiation' my life felt changed in ways that are hard to describe. All I can say is that my intuitive abilities improved and the number of daily synchronicities increased enormously.

We may be still in the Stone Age as far as scientifically understanding these subtle vibratory attunements, but there is plenty of anecdotal evidence. Healers have often talked of synchronizing vibrations between two people, or between people and crystals, or people and external unseen energies. Different crystals are thought to embody energies, or we could say strings, vibrating at different frequencies. When placed on parts of the body, these frequencies in the crystal synchronize with that particular body vibration. If the body part has lowered energy or the particular rhythm/oscillation has slowed down or become too variable, the crystal will bring it back into harmony.

1. The Magic Vortex

Psychics have talked of the vortexes of energy that can be experienced in magical groups as well as individually. During meditation I have often experienced my head moving automatically round and round in a kind of spiral movement. It feels as though an external force is winding out and into me. There is a calm and almost ecstatic sensation attached to this experience. I have also experienced the movement of energy winding into vortex shapes through group magical work.

One hot, lazy day a group of us went to the woods to carry out a magical ceremony for the summer solstice. The procession of 13 people set out from the main road plunging away from the sound of traffic down a narrow, leafy lane. We all had ivy draped round our heads, behind our ears, over our shoulders. Some of us were wearing jeans and T-shirts. Others were in flowing white robes and jangling bracelets that broke the silence as we walked. One young man with dreadlocks walked barefoot. It was both a mad midsummer outing and a serious ritual procession.

Eventually we arrived at the clearing where sun still flickered through the leaves. The old oaks seemed pleased we had come. A circle just seemed to happen spontaneously. There were no leaders and everyone had a role. Some were there to create the sacred space. One older woman in black used a wand to mark out an imaginary circle around the outside of the group. Four young women faced the four directions of north, south, east and west, and opening their arms to the sky they called for the energies of each place to arrive. Gods and goddesses and other energies were invoked. Then webs of red thread were woven between everyone, songs were sung, promises were made, gifts were offered. Just before the end we began a slow chant that turned into a deep 'arhhhhh' sound from our bellies. As it got louder and louder, the energy in the circle began to spin. It went round and round like a vortex, starting broad at the bottom and spiralling to a point above our heads. We had formed a cone of energy to send out to people who needed healing, and to add to the positive, peaceful energy on the earth. Afterwards we took some of it into ourselves and closed the sacred circle.

This vortex of spinning energy takes the same shape as the spinning strings being discovered by physicists. It has been familiar to white witches, shamans, mystics and psychics for thousands of years.

2. Yeats' Vortex Visions

A particularly interesting attempt to use the tension between opposites and the spinning vortex image for human development comes from the poet WB Yeats[8]. In *A Vision* he writes pages and pages of 'channelled' information from his wife. It came through as automatic writing in answer to Yeats' questions. The spirit guides' description of the other dimensions has some extraordinary similarities to those of string theory. They describe the main geometric form in unseen matter/energy as conical gyres often in pairs, one within the other, winding in opposite directions.

But the beings sending this information were most interested in how humans can grow and develop. 'It was part of their purpose to affirm that all the gains of man come from conflict with the opposite of his true being.' And this process happens on a soul level as well as in an individual's lifetime. Yeats quotes medieval descriptions of souls changing from gyre to sphere and back again. The sphere is seen as 'the final place of rest'. Swedenborg's mystical writings are also quoted. He describes 'two poles one opposite to the other ... in the form of cones.' Even Flaubert talked of the double cone and was going to include it in a story he never wrote called *La Spirale*.

In Yeats' *A Vision* there are several different pairs of opposites, described as Time and Space, Subjectivity and Objectivity, Will and Mask, Creative Mind and Body of Fate. Each opposite winds down into a point and back again, whirling in contrary directions. Yeats relates the different points of intersection to the phases of the moon, another rhythm. He also calls it the great wheel and links it to the dances of the Sufi whirling dervishes, those 'mysterious dancers who left the traces of their feet to puzzle the Caliph of Baghdad and his learned men'.

According to Yeats, this wheel is completed in every individual judgment throughout a whole lifetime. He even applies it to historical processes. This winding motion operates on many scales. Yeats saw it as a way of seeking and attaining the opposite and then returning to the original, but always further on in the spiral. Every phase of growth and change is in itself a wheel. 'The individual soul is awakened by a violent oscillation.' He quotes the poet Verlaine oscillating between the church and the brothel ... 'until it sinks in on that Whole where the contraries are united, the antinomies resolved'.

This is exactly the same kind of process we have been exploring in this book, whereby we try to live more rhythmically, fully expressing both sides of ourselves to bring the opposites together. This is how we come to live more in the flow. We can do this consciously or unconsciously. It can happen to us without our will, as these natural forces in different dimensions spin through and around us. Or we can use our will to align ourselves consciously with the process.

118

3. Individual Soul Magic

If we choose to work consciously with our own rhythmic soul process, we need to work out the scale or level of the rhythms, oscillations or vortex windings that we want to attune to. If these are on the psychological and soul levels, we are generally talking about unseen rhythms. We may be able to work out through intuition and imagination what our main opposite issues are. Do we have conflicts between sexuality and spirituality, caring for others and self interest, independence and dependence, pride and humility ? It may be that on the soul level these rhythmic processes between all the opposites work themselves out through many lifetimes, not just one. People who recall different past lives often find that they go in pairs of opposites. Yeats writes that, 'The souls of victim and tyrant are bound together and, unless there is a redemption through the intercommunication of the living and the dead, that bond may continue life after life... till the expiation is completed and the oscillation brought to an end for each at the same moment. There are other bonds, master and servant, benefactor and beneficiary, any relation that is deeper than the intellect may become such a bond.'

Roger Woolger[9] a Jungian psychotherapist has also shown that the pattern of the soul's journey through past lives follows the 'law of opposites'. He gives many examples of people remembering completely opposite past lives. A young man re-experienced several lives as a cruel warrior, but then one as a very gentle woman. In the therapy work he gradually became more accepting of the gentle side of himself. But he could also accept the warrior side as being a part of him too. The opposites may start off being very far apart, with wild swings between them, but through working with equalizing rhythms and consciously experiencing both extremes, they become closer. Living rhythmically is being with the natural flow between opposites that are close and interconnected, rather than split wide apart.

A client called Jackie came with some experience of working with past lives. She had had a past life recollection of having been a spiritual leader in a very ancient Middle Eastern city. Her first knowledge of this was in a dream in which she was climbing up a spiral staircase in a tall tower made of mud. There were windows on each floor. But as she looked out onto the city below through one window after another, it changed dramatically each time. On awaking Jackie realized that she was seeing the same place, but at different times. The spiral shape is once again present. Later in a 'memory' of one lifetime there, she had been taken out side the city wall and stoned to death because of a betrayal. This helped her understand her fear of crowds and of being in a powerful position. It seemed that she had betrayed the whereabouts of the most sacred posses-sions of her tribe to an outsider. He was a handsome man that she had fallen in love with. In this life she had been unable to commit to any man as she was unconsciously afraid of the wrath of the community. Yet she had always been attracted to men from different backgrounds. Jackie felt disrespected and undervalued for her spiritual power this lifetime. It was an opposite experience to the many times she had been in an elevated position. But perhaps it was vital for her soul's journey that she let the ego go. Eventually Jackie stopped needing that recognition and could take her place as a healer without having such fear of the crowd. She could accept both the spiritual side and the ordinary human side that wanted a relationship. She could be both a separate individual and part of a community.

It seems as though on a soul level there is a 'force' trying to balance all the opposites in human nature. Perhaps as souls evolve there is a closer connection between all the opposites and a flow through them all at higher and higher speeds. It appears as though this leads to a deeper freedom to be both everything and nothing. Ancient initiations and experiences like that of the Buddha getting enlightened, often involve facing the very worst opposite of human nature. The Buddha faced all the 'demons' and temptations known to humanity while sitting under the Bodi tree to get enlightened. We can all be murderers or tyrants, terrorists or simply nasty little bullies, given the right circumstances. Somehow it seems that the soul's consciousness knows this, and needs to experience the opposites. Different individuals appear to have different sets of opposites to work through. For some it is to do with power. After being powerful in past lives, and perhaps misusing that power, a soul may have to experience extreme powerlessness. Most people who recall past lives seem to have been both men and woman. In patriarchal cultures, that could in itself lead to experiences of relative powerfulness and power-lessness.

Another Jungian, James Hillman[10] shows how much more useful rhythmic images of consciousness are. 'Hierarchical models require the inferiority of lower positions. But we can experience and conceive consciousness by means of other images. For example, rather than super-imposed levels, we might speak of circulation and rotation, of the comings and goings of flow.' He adds, 'In this structure all positions are occasionally inferior, and no positions are ever finally inferior.' He argues that we need to trust this flow that will develop automatically. He calls it the urge of the process itself: what goes up will come down. For him the going down is just as important as the heroic going up. He emphasizes a trust in the process itself without needing too much conscious will.

However, given Western culture's hierarchical thinking, we need to make a more conscious effort to emphasize the downward, the dark or indeed any opposite that is perceived as inferior. We can intend to align ourselves with what nature is trying to rebalance. It is likely to take an enormous effort of will to do or think the opposite of what our culture is telling us. This is where the healthy rebel comes in.

I have personally rebelled most of my life to rebalance in favor of the deep feminine. In 1970s feminist conferences I would be the only one wearing a dress. For a year I led a group based on the mysteries of Rhea. We worked with the idea of 'endarkenment' rather than enlightenment. There was a black veiled figure on the altar representing the 'Old Ones'. We visualized meditating in dark deep caves and becoming nothing. In rituals I would cover my head with the black veil, reclaiming it for spiritual growth, loss of ego and deep respect for the dark feminine. At a ceremony to celebrate becoming post-menopausal, I veiled myself and all my friends and family came to give me blessings. Only a few found it too weird to join in!

Can Rhythm Heal Splits in the World Soul?

As well as individual souls, there seem to be group souls, and even the world soul, or anima mundi. After 9/11, Deepak Chopra, the popular new age guru, wrote that there must be a deep split in the world soul. The powerfulness of America contrasts with the relative powerlessness of the rest of the world. That extreme hierarchical split manifests in smaller ones everywhere, even deep inside our psyche. The hierarchic model runs the world. Perhaps the rhythm model can help toward healing these splits, over time. Empires rise and fall. The oppressed react. Those who are high eventually become low. The rhythm model can be applied to specific examples of the crisis we face today. For example, the present flight into fundamentalism in the major world religions seems to come from fear of an uncertain post-modern world and the increased power of women. But the desire to equalize is there too. Islamic academics have written of 'the rage for equality'. War is the terrorism of the rich, terrorism is the war of the poor.

Using the rhythm model it is possible to find the connection between different faiths, find commonalities and a deep equality. In 2005 I was personally involved in making links between Islam and Paganism in a variety of contexts. My deepest experience of this was with a close friend and soul mate, as two individuals, tuning deeply into the world soul. It was at a time when the perceived opposition between Islam and the West seemed particularly acute. He is a Sufi who came from a Kashmiri community in Yorkshire UK and I too was born in Yorkshire to English parents. As I am an older feminist pagan we might have seemed too different to connect spiritually at the depth we did. Yet my young Muslim friend and I had far more in common than we had differences. There was agreement on important issues. We both felt that there is a need to bring the sacred dimension back into the forefront of a world gone crazy in its worship of the market as god. We both believed in the progressive values of equality and justice. We were both sensitive to the energies of place and have had personal ecstatic experiences of some kind of divine connection. I believe that most of what we personally shared is shared by most of humanity. All of us share conscious or unconscious attunement to rhythms of the moon and sun, seen and unseen, inside us and outside. Humans made spiritual connections with these rhythmic patterns in nature long before any of the main religions of today began. This 'natural' spirituality has never completely died out in Islam or any other mainstream religions.

After months of discussion and sharing we drove together one overcast Saturday afternoon, high onto the Derbyshire moors to visit the 'Stonehenge' of the North at Arbor Lowe. This massive circular earthwork was built in around 2500 BC. Like a giant clock, enormous fallen stones marked the hours around the inside and formed two hands in the center. Frozen in time it still ticks to a long forgotten rhythm up there on the moors. We came like pilgrims through the ages to honor the stones, the place, the energy, and the symbolic meaning of the circle.

Once tribal peoples may have circled round and round, imitating the cycles of the sun and moon and sharing a sense of deep equality. It could be seen as the same motion as the electrons winding around the protons on a sub atomic level. Indeed it is the same spinning movement of the superstrings and the vortexes of energy described above. And like those minute electrons, we processed round and round, leaving hardly any mark on the springy green turf. Walking slowly in meditative concentration, it felt as though we were suddenly and mysteriously transported spinning through time and space to the deserts of Arabia. We saw thousands of humans dressed in white, circling the ancient Kaaba in Mecca. Everyone was swirling round this other ancient stone, men and women, of all races and ages. There was a profound sense of equality and of the connect-edness with nature.

It seemed as though this was something that humans have been doing for hundreds of thousands of years. And while in the West, such rituals have long been forgotten, in Arabia they are still being performed in the 21st century. Circulating the Kaaba preserves a ritual going back to prehistoric times. As we swirled with them and watched as if from the sky, a flock of swallows began spiralling above our heads. Then we were drawn back to the central stones and sat for what seemed like hours, lost in the emptiness and openness of silent meditation. Finally we whirled together round and round, keeping our feet on one spot, arms in the air, like the famous Sufi whirling dervishes. Like them we were using our bodies to link heaven and earth in the basic spinning movements that string theorists now see as at the heart of nature. We became as one in the rhythm.

Things to do: Working with Nature

1. Spend time alone in nature. Experience yourself as an equal part of nature. Empty your mind to be purely receptive to the energies around you. See what she has to teach you personally. Are there any meaningful synchronicities, like animals or birds appearing as signs. Take some paper and pencils with you to sit with a favorite tree or plant and just look at it for half an hour first. Then draw it, without worrying about being realistic or artistic.

2. Work out what you can personally do to help the rebalancing needed for human survival on this planet. What can you recycle? How can you cut down energy consumption? Be realistic, and don't feel guilty if you can't do it all.

3. On a soul level, think about what seem to be the main sets of opposites affecting your life. Get past life readings, so you can link themes in the present to those of the past. Where there seems to be a one sidedness or too big a swing from one opposite to the other, work out

where you need to put more energy. Do you need to let go of a past life that is still blocking your flow today?

4. On the level of the world soul, think about what contribution you might be able to make to rebalance opposites in the world as a whole.

5. Practice raising sexual energy alone or with a partner. Squeeze pelvic muscles, visualize exciting situations, stay still and let go inside. Follow where it leads you.

6. Visualize patterns of vortexes and spirals in the air around you. Draw them.

CHAPTER SEVEN

PSYCHO-RHYTHMS

Can psychotherapy and counseling help us to dare to surrender control and trust equalizing rhythms to flow through us? What aspects of traditional psychotherapy help or hinder us in letting the healthy inner rebel out to dance? And how can we move from being stuck with layer upon layer of inner hierarchies to the freedom of living rhythmically? I have suggested exercises and given examples of rhythmic living in previous chapters, but this is a difficult and life long process and it is often helpful to have a guide, a supporter, a witness at certain times. Sometimes this person can be a psychotherapist or a counselor. At other times it could be a teacher or friend, or someone you meet on a train. I don't believe that formal counseling or psychotherapy is essential. All of life can be personal development and therapy. But as I work as a psychotherapist this final chapter explores how equalizing rhythms are being used in this field.

Jungian Rhythms and Freudian Hierarchies

Psychotherapy has a history of aiming to dissolve rigid defenses, heal hierarchical splits in the psyche and generally balance the opposites within. Carl Jung is the name most often associated with opposites in human psychology. His writings have a deep sense of the power and importance of the flow between them, at least in the psyche. He quotes 'Old Heraclitus' and describes him as 'a very great sage, (who) discovered the most marvelous of all psychological laws; the regulative function of opposites ... a running contrariwise, by which he meant that sooner or later everything runs into its opposite.'[1]

Jung did however perceive opposites, like all of us, from his own limited, historically bound frame of reference. One example is his idea of a feminine anima (soul) to balance the male self, and a masculine animus (spirit) to balance the female self. Today such ideas are criticized for being too simplistic.

He also had a strong sense of the psychological importance of balance. For example, he would argue that a person who was too obsessed with the intellect might find that their neglected emotional side will hold them back in their life's journey. They might fall passionately in love with someone who does not even notice they exist. Or they might have uncontrollable rages that frighten everyone away. In some way or another the 'inferior' opposite finds its way of being noticed.

Jung believed that dreams were often compensatory. For example, dreaming of being a king could provide an opposite experience for a person with feelings of worthlessness and powerlessness. Jung saw life energy or libido as flowing between opposite poles. He saw the psyche as a dynamic system in constant self-regulating movement. The greater the tension between the opposites, the greater the energy. When one extreme is reached, libido passes into its opposite. Violent rage turns suddenly to calm. Progression leads to regression. Other opposites that Jung used a lot were the self and the shadow, thinking and feeling, sensation and intuition, introvert and extrovert, conscious and unconscious, masculine and feminine.

In Jungian psychology one aim is to make all these processes conscious and to work actively in therapy to balance the opposites. A very macho man might see a very feminine figure in a dream. In therapy he would be encouraged to see her as an anima figure to befriend, to 'talk' to, and get to know consciously. Active imagination might be used to visualize this figure intentionally, and even paint her. But James Hillman, who is a Jungian therapist, has an even stronger sense of trusting the balancing processes to do their work even without our conscious attention. Hillman even gave up being a therapist at one point, and argued that there is no need to analyze dreams. Simply having them is enough. There is a kind of mystical surrender in Hillman's thinking that does not need too much ego control. 'We are obliged to trust Eros' (another name for equalizing rhythms) ... the urge of the process itself.'

Perhaps the opposites never need to be finally integrated. Any image of a final solution seems problematic in this post-modern world. The intention can be more to see and accept all the opposites, and free them from a vertical, rigid connection to a fluid one. For some people the problem can be too much swing from one opposite to the other, as in bi-polar mental illness. For them, the opposites need to be brought closer together so that there is a gentle dance between them. A

Play of Opposites from Art Therapy

person can feel comfortable being a bit sad and then a bit happy, rather than manic one day and suicidal the next (although some people perhaps like the intensity of wild swings). But neither of these aims is about merging the opposites into one, or creating a permanent static pattern of relationship implied by the images of mandalas, so beloved of Jungians. Opposites here are given equal value, but they are stuck: circles in squares, triangles in circles.

Freud had an even more hierarchical model of the psyche in which the Id, or instincts were to be controlled by the superior Ego. 'Where Id was, there ego shall be. It is work of culture.' He believed that the wild Id of nature must be conquered by the rational forces of the ego. Native peoples, children and women have often been associated with nature and the id, while white men are seen as more like the rational ego. While both Jung and Freud use dualistic opposites in their models, Jung intercon-nects them equally, while Freud puts one above and in charge of the other.

In their brilliant book on *The Cultural Basis of Racism and Group Oppression* Hodge, Stuckman and Trost[2] show how Freud's underlying hierarchical paradigm plays a large, but hidden part in social inequality. The image of control and power over is deeply embedded in Freudian thought. 'Psychoanalysis is an instrument to enable the ego to achieve a progressive conquest of the Id.' Note the word conquest.

A depressed 45-year-old Vietnamese client called Su had been to see a Freudian analyst for two years. As the youngest daughter of the family she was expected to care for the others as well as make a good marriage. A strong sense of duty was installed. But Su had rebelled. The expected dependency had turned into a brutal independence. She was a successful journalist with no desire to marry. This was interpreted by the Freudian analyst as a defence against the longing for mother love. Her rebellious refusal to accept the interpretations was seen as Su not allowing the analyst to feed her. While there may be grains of truth in this, it was only when she was fully accepted and respected for her choices, through rhythm therapy, that she came out of depression. In her own way Su was equalizing her opposites. From being deeply disrespected in her culture she needed the opposite, full respect. She did not always want to be infantilized. After a lifetime of being expected to fulfil duties, she needed to follow her own inner wisdom. From being told what to do, she needed to follow her own deep intuition. After using her head to solve all problems, she rejected over intellectual interpretations. Su needed to trust the rhythms of her Id not to control it even more.

Post Jungians such as Andrew Samuels argue for pluralism, stating that this is 'an anti-hierarchical attitude'[3]. But without an explicit commitment to equalizing, the different parts or sides can all too often rearrange themselves into new hierarchies. In the world of psychotherapy, lip service is often paid to the pluralistic value of all kinds of approaches, but its social reality actually gives psychoanalysis much higher status. And it is a lot more expensive than most other therapies. All sides of the individual can be theoretically valued equally, but reason really still

reigns supreme. For example, Cognitive Behavioral Therapy, which is entirely based on the use of reason to overcome problems, is increasingly popular.

Oliver James, a clinical psychologist, has been arguing for years that the hierarchies of the win/lose culture are psychologically disastrous. In his latest book *Affluenza*[4] he describes the increasing obsession with keeping up with the Joneses, materially, as a damaging motivation for life. Instead he advocates developing the ability to act for the intrinsic value of the task in hand. Then it is no longer important what status it will bring. Interestingly, in relation to this book, he calls this 'being in the flow'.

Erich Fromm[5] was a Freudian, but with a strong sense of the problems of inner hierarchy. He wrote of the marketing personality who is always working out the cost benefits of any relationship. The inner judge starts measuring the other person in a vertical way, from the minute they meet. What value do they have? Can they give me something I want, or not? He advocated mature loving from the core of oneself instead. Fromm also contrasted our extreme 'having' culture with the equally important approach of 'being' in the flow.

Humanistic Rhythms in Psychotherapy

Humanistic psychology grew up in the 1960s greatly influenced by Eastern philosophies of non dualism and the interconnection of opposites. In Gestalt psychology there is a particular emphasis on opposites. They use techniques that work with opposite sides of the self, such as Top dog and Underdog. The aim is for the two sides to see and hear each other fully, and then have a dialogue. Often clients are encouraged to act out, draw or experience being both sides. When two chairs are used to represent the two opposites, the person literally moves from one to the other, backwards and forwards in a rhythm. Here again there is an equalizing rhythm going on consciously and unconsciously in the therapy.

However, there can be a very hierarchical relationship between the directive Gestalt therapist and their client. The founder Fritz Perls seems to have been a very dominating and hierarchical character, while the founder of Person Centered Therapy, Carl Rogers[6] was apparently a much more respectful and gentle man. His approach emphasizes equal power relationships in the therapy or counseling situation. The equalizing rhythms are between the two people with neither fully in control. The therapist is there to create the best conditions for the client's natural self-regulating mechanisms to work. Rogers described these as coming from the natural organismic self. Like Hillman, he had more trust in the person's own rhythmic, balancing mechanisms.

In many ways, Person Centered Psychotherapy and Counseling is the most rhythmic and non-hierarchical of all the approaches. Power relations are looked at and the values of deep equality are explicit as well as implicit in the teaching. The therapist can always imagine themselves in the same place as the client and does not take the role of superior expert. The client is generally followed rather than led. John Rowan, a humanistic psychotherapist, writes in his important book *Ordinary Ecstasy*, 'More and more research findings have piled up to show that hierarchy does harm to people.' [7]

But there can be a subtle hierarchy in the idea of personal development where individuals are encouraged to climb ladders of self fulfilment to higher and higher states of happiness and satisfaction. This ever-upward ascent is often totally individualistic. It can take place with no regard for social and economic inequalities or environmental issues. Techniques from humanistic psychology have been used to humanize capitalism by helping people get happier at work, whatever that work happens to be. It could be working for oil companies that oppress people in Nigeria or almost any business that puts profit before human need. And most of them do.

Therapy can even help rather than hinder the economic status quo. It helps create more and more, increasingly demanding, capitalist consumers searching for self-fulfilment. The corporate world relies on people's basic dissatisfaction with themselves as they are. Now people want to buy experience as well as goods, creating the vast tourist industry and yet more inequality in the world. Too often, in the therapy world, there is a blindness to the bigger picture. Because rhythmic therapy is about balancing the opposites in all areas and on all levels, including society and the environment, it looks at consequences of actions in terms of inequality.

This broader aim conflicts with much of the consumerist language of many personal development gurus. The ignoring of global inequalities leaves a wide spiritual hole at the very center of so much teaching today. All those inspirational seminars, books and videos that help you to believe in yourself, encourage success regardless of wider issues. Some even explicitly speak of material success. Some tell us we can get anything we want if we visualize it often enough. This desired thing is as likely to be a particular car, a bigger apartment or a partner. Yet still, as James Oliver showed in his book Affluenza, many rich people are deeply unhappy. They are not living in the flow. Nor are they helping to balance up the bigger opposites in the split and damaged world we all share.

Ruth, a 25-year-old, had always been driven to succeed. She expected to get straight A's for everything at school and then at college. At first she simply switched the same pattern of behavior to her personal development. Ruth went to workshops almost every weekend. Her apartment was overflowing with self help books. Lists of helpful thoughts and things to do each day covered her fridge. It was when she began telling her friends what they should be doing with their lives, that Ruth realized there was a problem. They began getting angry with her. She was shocked at first, convinced that it was the others who just weren't ready for her wonderful advice. She was superior and good and only trying to help.

Rhythm therapy started with the issue of superiority, helping her see that it came from a deeper feeling of not being good enough herself. She was always hoping that the next workshop or book would make her a better person. It seemed as though she wasn't good enough just as she was. Gradually through weekly sessions of therapy, during which there was a basic acceptance of her simply in her being, Ruth changed. No demands were made on her. Silence sometimes happened for a while. One day she curled up like a baby. Another day we meditated together. Feeling equal in the therapy helped her see others as equal, even if they didn't go to the gym or read self help books. Ruth also started reading more about the wider world, from a progressive point of view. As she began to see the bigger picture, and consumed less and less, Ruth became more satisfied with herself. She found peace in a simpler life and a loving relationship with someone very different.

Rhythmic Therapy

There are a number of criteria that can be applied to any therapy situation to see if it is rhythmic or hierarchical, adding to the inequalities in the world or helping to change them. Rhythmic therapy is not so much one particular new technique as a new paradigm for personal and social change. It is not so much a new school of therapy as a new approach to all schools of therapy. It is not so much a new method as a new intention, with the aim of equalizing.

1. The first aim is to clear out serious emotional problems in order to make room for a clear attunement to the needs of each moment. When we are deeply attuned, our actions and words flow with the balancing, equalizing forces of whatever situations we find ourselves in. The intention is to create an empty vessel for natural energy to flow through more freely. Relief from the misery of the problems is important, but it is not the only goal.

2. The rhythmic approach appreciates that all kinds of therapy have their advantages and disadvantages, depending on what a particular person needs. Today there is often a hierarchy in the field, with psychoanalysis at the top and person centered counseling at the bottom. This can put the status and cost of therapy before the deeper needs of the individual. The rhythmic approach does not see any one technique or type

of therapy as above or ultimately better than another. It is a matter of trusting intuition as well as reason, and of finding the right therapist and approach for anyone seeking help.

3. To be a rhythmic therapist, it helps to be trained in a range of therapeutic skills, so you can chose what is most appropriate for each particular person. These can include psychodynamic, person centered, Jungian and cognitive approaches. Important skills include empathic listening and feeding back to the client what they have said, to show that they have been heard; loving attention and full acceptance of the person; holding the space and making it safe with clear boundaries; paying attention to the unconscious patterns such as transference and counter transference, defences and projections; diagrams to explain patterns such as divisions of inner opposites like 'perfect' and 'worthless'; dream interpretation with the client's help; and creative techniques such as Gestalt chair work, art therapy, active imagination.

4. There is a deep and genuine respect for the person, however troubled they are. The core of the human being can be valued, whatever they have done. This sense can be experienced by therapists from any tradition. Deep equality comes from the feeling of two vulnerable and complex humans in a room together. Neither is ultimately superior.

5. We see ourselves as co-creators in a rhythmic equalizing process that goes on between two souls interacting. Psychotherapy literally means soul healing. The psyche is the soul, and it may be split hierarchically with an unacceptable inferior side. It seems that souls 'want' to heal themselves. We can help this process but not dictate it. The rhythmic therapist creates a sacred space and time to allow the transformation to happen in its own flow. You cannot push the river.

6. The equalizing of opposites within the psyche and outside in the world, is the background framework, underlying everything that happens. Sometimes this is consciously expressed. At other times this equalizing process is unconscious. Hierarchical structures of thought can be addressed consciously or dissolved unconsciously through the

New Rhythms of Success and Failure

transforming process. Healthy rebellion is encouraged. Even in the therapeutic relationship, a client may need to trust her own intuition, rather than be told what to do or think, even when the therapist has a valid interpretation. Her rebellion is not analyzed away, for example, as only being about transference onto a bossy mother figure.

7. There is no hierarchical division between success and failure. The therapy process is itself in the flow, organically evolving without outside control. Measurement and evaluation are not part of this process. There can be client goals or intentions to be clarified near the beginning and maybe from time to time later. But they are not constantly referred to and measured. Rather they are put into the 'hands' of the flow, and then left to play themselves out.

Victimhood and Rhythms of Change

One of the problems associated with facing hierarchies is that people think it only means connecting with the pain of being a victim. Many women reacted against feminist therapy because they felt that it encouraged us to feel like permanent victims in a patriarchal society, always on the bottom of the hierarchy. Women have rightly focused on empowering themselves, in a world where power means taking the opposite position to the victim. However this horror of being an inferior victim has sometimes led to a massive denial of the realities of patriarchy. There is still a vertical division in the minds and deep unconscious structures of most humans that puts men and the masculine way of being on top. The problem is, what to do about it.

The rhythmic approach is to start by turning things upside down, and taking power. But then it involves loosening up the underlying structure, not simply becoming the persecutor or dominator in turn. It is both a refusal to be a victim and an awareness of the depth of the hierarchies in our heads and in the outside world. It is also about getting to know and feel comfortable with all the different roles, of power and power-lessness, leading and following, depending and nurturing. No role is permanently superior to another. The point is not to get stuck anywhere. The free person can rebel appropriately against inequality, rather than from a rigid victim position.

In Transactional Analysis there is a model of Victim, Persecutor, Rescuer. It can be helpful to work out which role a person is playing. People who see themselves as victims, often become persecutors in certain situations. On a global scale this can be seen in the very real victimhood of Jewish people leading to the Israeli State becoming a persecutor of others. But people who persecute or oppress are often reluctant to admit that they or their ancestors have played that role. It is not comfortable. It's much easier to feel like a victim. It seems to be an important stage in therapy to fully feel the sorrow of having been part of an oppressor group. I remember the overwhelming relief when a man first admitted to me that we do still live in a patriarchal society in which he has privilege simply for being a man. Until that kind of communication happens from the heart it is hard to really dialogue with the so-called 'other'.

Most of us are in denial most of the time. Men can be in denial of patriarchal realities. White people can be in denial of racism. Guilt can block honesty. For example, a black person may want to hear heartfelt pain from white people around the horrors of the slave trade. Instead she often gets excuses or embarrassment. Shame and guilt are not places to stay stuck in, but can be the beginning of equalizing responses to extreme oppression. Then there can be movement towards whatever is needed for wider equalizing processes such as an acknowledgement of the reality, dialogue and compassion. Individual therapy is a limited context, but the work we all do on our inner victim and our inner oppressor contributes to wider freedom and equality.

Rhythm therapy often starts with accepting and empowering a person in the present moment. It can have an intellectual component, as some people are helped by understanding the idea of hierarchy versus rhythm. But for people who are already too unbalanced towards the mind, this teaching would not be the first priority. It usually arises naturally. People talk about the different sides of themselves and can easily see these as vertically divided. One side is far above the other. I might use my arms stretched far apart to demonstrate this model. Or we might draw it. And using the arms again, I can demonstrate what it looks like to let these sides flow. Clients increasingly talk about wanting to be in the flow, without any prompting from me. So the ideas tend to follow organically from their experiences. The rhythm model is not superimposed from the top, but grows out of our co-creation.

David, a 53-year-old man, came to therapy for depression. A tall and awkward form folded himself into the chair opposite me. He wanted to know what models I was using straight away. His serious balding head led the way and leaned towards me, wanting to know, to control through knowing. I could see that there was already a hierarchy between his mind and body. The body seemed like an afterthought dragged along by the dominant mind.

After explaining the rhythm model and the way I work, I asked for his life story. David had grown up in Brooklyn, New York. His Jewish parents had emigrated from Lithuania. They struggled with a small laundry business and wanted more for their son. His mother especially, acutely aware of the race and money hierarchies, was determined to climb the social ladder. She pushed her son to work his little socks off at school. David remembers feeling different because of his relative poverty and his

Jewishness. But he was also exceptionally bright. When he eventually went to college David hoped that he would be with more like-minded people. But there the money hierarchy still reigned supreme. There was a deep sense of unconscious shame at his roots that took us months of therapy to discover. His superior mind overcame this feeling of inferiority. For a while he was a Marxist lecturing in a prestigious college on politics and economics. Then he became a consultant economist advising the Democrat party. It was always up, up and up till his second wife left him. David said that he couldn't understand why she had gone.

In therapy much of the work was encouraging David to inhabit his body in the present moment. He did not feel basically loveable in his being. Life had all been about thinking and doing. The opposites of being and feeling were firmly suppressed. The shame and pain from childhood were too unbearable to feel at first. It took years of simply being fully with him in the room, for his heart to begin to melt. Because of buried feelings of inferiority and victim hood he had become 'superior'. David was always trying to challenge me and could not at first be 'fed' by my words or heart connection.

Only once he had let me in could I encourage him to think differently about everything but especially himself. We moved from hierarchic thinking in which the world was divided between superior and inferior, persecutor and victim, to rhythmic structures of thought. He related them to Dialectics and Taoism, finding the new idea interesting intellectually as well as emotionally. His core self esteem was raised slowly and painfully, with visits to his childhood and to the massive legacy of the Holocaust. With the help of meditation as well, David also began to live more in the present moment and trust the flow of life as it happens. His need to control everything with his 'superior' mind gradually changed by developing an ability to also listen to his intuition. Then one day David took up dancing.

Seeing life in terms of rigid vertical divisions that need changing to ever fluid horizontal ones is a kind of cognitive therapy. But instead of seeing the client's thinking as irrational and needing to be made more rational, it is about a totally different structure of thought. The rhythm versus hierarchy model is a way of defining and describing problems. The solution is not just thinking more rationally as in cognitive behavioral thrapy. Rather it is in switching to a totally different paradigm. The opposites are pictured as flowing rather than as vertically and permanently divided.

Anna, 38, arrived to see me elegantly dressed with a haughty look of challenging superiority. Was I going to be up to the job of working with her? She asked me lots of questions about my experience and qualifications on that first session. She was born in Saudi Arabia but had lived in the US for 20 years, since arriving to study chemistry. Her father seemed to have been particularly keen for his daughter to succeed academically as well as her two brothers. She was close to him but rather scornful of her mother. Her father had a vast library of books at home and inspired Anna to go to University to study chemistry. Yet secretly Anna dreamt of being a writer. She wanted to write about the complex interrelations between the different hierarchies that have shaped her. There was the general inferiority of women, despite her particularly enlightened father. Then there was the sense of isolation and inferiority of her whole community in a foreign country. But there were also the class hierarchies within the US Arab community, in which her family were situated rather precariously in the middle, as fairly successful business people. Above them was the vast and wealthy Saudi royal family. Below them was everyone else. Their Filipino servants were seen as particularly low status. Anna felt intuitively that they were not treated properly, but reasoned that it was normal. When young, she had never dared to trust her intuition, seeing it as inferior and feminine.

Anna had initially rebelled against her own culture including its Islamic religion. She was part of a Westernized middle class and had refused to have an arranged marriage, to her mother's distress but with her father's tacit support. At University she met and married a Saudi man who came from an academic atheist family. They had two children and seemed to be the perfect family. But Anna became depressed and felt something was missing from her life. Then she started having extraordinary dreams of angels trying to show her a hidden path along a strange and magical river. Anna had always secretly believed that there was a spiritual reality outside the science that her father and husband had encouraged her to prioritize. Reason had seemed so superior to the intuition and to what she perceived as superstition that her mother believed in.

This conflict was still going on in her mind when Anna came to see me. There was a suspicion that I was one of those irrational spiritual women that she still half despised. I wondered why she had come to see a woman. But somewhere deep in the unconscious was a desire to reclaim that other side of herself. I encouraged her to start writing a dream journal. We used guided imagery in our sessions, starting with a point in the dream like a path and imaging where it might lead to. This process opened up her unconscious creativity to rebalance the one-sided nature of her previous life. She began writing short stories about her community and finally got one published. Anna also worked on her relationship with 'the despised mother' and began to accept and value her.

In Rhythm therapy, eventually the 'other' becomes equalized and dissolves into the self. To begin with, in our thinking the other is often below us. We are the norm and they are the inferior other. It is vital to acknowledge honestly all our projections in the first stages of transformation. This can be a very uncomfortable process. Although racism has declined globally in recent years, there is still a long way to go. And it can be subtle and unconscious.

Having grown up in colonial Africa, I had a lot of projections onto black people in general. Mostly these were positive but seriously stereotyped. They could dance and I couldn't. They were spiritually powerful and I wasn't. They were closer to the earth. The 'other' represented what I unconsciously lacked. As I became more whole, I had less need to project. Then one day I remember sitting in my kitchen, with a close black male friend. He happened to be a media studies lecturer, so knew all about concepts of the other. This beautiful powerful man suddenly turned to me with a big grin, and said, 'You are just so other!' I immediately replied, 'But I don't feel other.' He laughed. 'Nobody does!' In that moment all my theoretical knowledge exploded into a deep lived experience and I understood properly for the first time.

Some white people who care about injustice see the 'other' primarily as a victim. Sometimes guilt leads to patronizing attitudes and not giving valid criticism to someone simply because they are black, or brown. All action against inequality is vital, but there are deeper levels of consciousness and unconsciousness about otherness that need exploring. One way is to take back our projections and see what it is inside us that we are putting on to the 'other'. My stereotyped racist projection that black people have rhythm led me eventually to write this book and find the rhythm in me and in life. I also learnt to dance. Common negative projections include seeing the 'other' as dirty, aggressive or ignorant. We can put our own shadow fears on to the other, as well as our unexpressed positive sides.

Julie, 59, is a beautiful, large, white woman who arrived at her first session looking confident on the surface, with short dark hair, wearing a brightly colored kaftan and big dangling earrings. She had been feeling depressed and wondered whether it was the menopause or if there were more long-term and deep seated reasons. Julie had particularly wanted to see a feminist therapist. She felt that many of her problems related to the patriarchal society in which we live. Julie had campaigned for many feminist issues all her life. She is passionate about injustice and is still angry about all the different hierarchies in the world. From her teens in the 1970s onwards, she had rebelled against the society, and her parents. They were left wing academics who had subtly pressurized her to succeed at school on the one hand while pretending they did not care on the other. She had always secretly felt inferior to them and to her more academic older brother despite all the encouragement she got for her art. Julie dropped out of the art college she had so wanted to attend. She complained bitterly about the sexism and was ignored. The tutors only supported the male students doing abstract work. They ridiculed Julie's more figurative work and undermined her fragile confidence. For many years she gave up painting all together.

She trained in Teaching English as an Other Language and enjoyed working with people from many different countries, aware of all the different hierarchies involved. Politically she was active in socialist, feminist groups and had been deeply committed to the anti apartheid struggle. It was at one of their meetings that she met a brilliant and handsome African jazz musician called Joe. It was love at first sight. She talked about him with a starry, faraway look in her eyes. He represented both the exotic 'other' and the creative side, she had suppressed. They had ended up living together for seven years. Yet all of that time at home, there was an endless struggle for equality. Eventually she left, unable to cope with the drinking that came from his political frustration and life long experience of racism. He seemed to have been the love of her life. Since then she had not had a long-term relationship.

Julie had a fiercely independent side with a hidden terror of any dependency at all. It was as if depending on someone would destroy her. From an early age she had realized that emotional dependence on cold and distant parents was too painful. She created a situation with Joe where she always had more money than him. He was also unreliable. Dependence was not an option, so she would have an excuse not to experience its pain. Much of the work was to get the opposites of dependence and independence more balanced. She came to therapy twice a week for two years, and eventually allowed a degree of dependence and trust that had never been part of her life before. Julie's internal hierarchies were explored and this led to an understanding of her low self esteem. Everyone else had seemed 'higher' than she was. As Julie's confidence increased she began to paint again. At first another inner hierarchy appeared that was about perfection. She either had to be perfect or she felt completely worthless. But eventually she was able to just paint as an expression of feeling, and not mind if the end product was not 'perfectly balanced'. She was in the flow while painting.

Julie was still very angry with men and the patriarchy. But she began to also see her anger as an excuse not to trust in relationships. First she had to trust the flow of life, which in turn helped towards eventually developing a new relationship. She liked the sexual tension between men and women, but her healthy rebel hated the arrogance and superiority still in many men's unconscious minds. She felt that men weren't changing fast enough, but this no longer made her personally feel like a victim. It was just the way things were at present. Julie continued to be active in supporting women's rights at home and abroad. The inner changes and new relationship didn't end her sense of social injustice. But now she acted from a place of knowing and loving instead of emotional pain.

An Equalizing Shift in Society

The paradigm shift from hierarchy to rhythm, verticality to endless inter dimensional fluidity, from power-over, dominator models to equalizing ones, needs to happen at all levels of society. It can affect the thinking of wise leaders everywhere, asking questions about whether any action increases or decreases equality rather than whether it helps their particular group win more power. Ideas of fairer wealth distribution used to be called Socialism. But for many this has become too infected with the old hierarchical structures of thought and power. Deeper change is needed as well. A complete shift in the human psyche, in the world soul and in the models of thinking we all learn from day one, could be a next step in our evolution. Many hope it will happen naturally through mass awakening, spiritual revolution or even after a catastrophic disaster. But we could progress consciously too. We could change our minds to fit with the equalizing flow of our heartfelt, deepest intuitions, and with the underlying rhythmic, vibrating, spinning and spiraling structures of nature. Attuning ourselves consciously to deep equalizing patterns, through action or thought lead us to being more fully in the flow. And as we have seen, being in the flow just happens to make us happy too.

This new model, paradigm, framework, philosophy can be used in the macrocosm of politics and economics and in the microcosm of daily life. We will all use it differently. But I am ending this book with a personal example of a day consciously lived in the flow of equalizing rhythms.

An Ordinary Day Lived Rhythmically

Wake up, half remembering a dream. Decide not to get up. Dream more important. Process dream for half an hour in bed, till need to go for a pee. Feel the energy all around me. Glide to the bathroom, flow to the window, see rain. Rain is beautiful. Remember to be grateful for being alive, my heart opens to the day. Don't feel like doing yoga but walk mindfully to the kitchen instead. Left foot, breathe in, right foot, breath out. Words in silent rhythm too. Rhea, Era, Right, left, in, out. The others have already left the house. They have different rhythms. Put kettle on. Minds hops off to plans for the day. Pour hot water into mug. Keep breathing. Notice he hasn't washed up the breakfast things. Cross, unfair. Is it because he's a man? Think about gender hierarchy. Back to body, eating breakfast, breathing, tasting.

Rain stops. Go out to shop. Bump into an old friend. She looks glamorous. And I'm wearing the 'wrong' clothes. Her up, me down. Feel envious. Me even more down. Hierarchy set up. Keep breathing. Back to body. Open heart, do really love her. Remember the misery of comparisons. Return home to work on computer. Immediately come across an article on envy, which is clearly my issue for the day. Think about another old friend who used to envy me. Phone rings. It's her, inviting me to a party. I'm scared to tell her about the good things I'm doing. Keep breathing. My fear helps preserve the hierarchy. Let fear go. Open heart, want to know all her news. She doesn't ask me how I am. But I tell her anyway. Keep breathing. I'm OK, and she's OK. Two ultimately equal beings. But I soon tell her I have to go.

Turn on the radio and of course there is a program about sibling rivalry. Keep breathing. Laugh. What absurd creatures we are. Have a 'chat' to Rhea before I leave for a meeting. I visualize her swirling energy flowing all round me protecting me and smiling at me. Keep saying her name as I walk down the damp street, looking at its unimaginable beauty. On public transport I'm still covered by Rhea's protection, until that is, I see ex-lover behind me. Keep breathing. Hierarchy pops up. He's an alpha male and I'm a nobody. Heart races. Protection forgotten. Keep breathing. He comes over. We talk. It's all very cool and friendly. He asks if I am busy. I remember to pull myself up and feel equal. No. I say, I don't like being too busy. I need time to sit and stare at trees.

Arrive at the meeting. Sit. Keep feet flat on floor. Ground. Breath. In, out. Yes, no. Speak, listen. Feel angry with woman doing too much talking. Not very equal. Try to persuade the silent ones to speak. No luck. Think they resent me trying to rescue them. Equalizing not working. Let anger float away. Try to trust the process. Keep breathing. Feel hungry. Think of future lunch. Come back to the present. Enjoy just breathing. Feel fulfilled in the here and now for a while.

Over lunch everyone is talking about house prices, real estate. Competitiveness jumps frantically around the room. Lots of hierarchies here. And these are alternative people who care about social injustice. Feel inferior and envious. Then remember it doesn't matter. In a thousand years time we'll all be dead and transformed, whatever grand apartments we have now. Led to shy young man in corner to talk to. Bit dull. Try to open heart. Must find something in common. At last find he like 1960s music. Phew! Keep breathing. Feet on ground. We part for lunch. In between talk, try to focus on each mouthful. Difficult. Get drawn outside by Rhea to the perfect spot in the vast garden to eat dessert mindfully. Later think that the flowers don't envy each other. They are just being what they are.

Go back for more meetings and client sessions. In the flow, till I realize I've been overlooked for an upcoming conference. Feel hurt at lack of recognition. Me down, them up. Remember the rhythm of praise and blame, success and failure, being ignored and being attended to. It doesn't matter in the great rhythms of life. Go to park. Walk along path saying to myself praise... blame, praise, blame, right foot, praise, left foot blame. After a while it really doesn't matter. Back in flow. Meet a child and a cat who are just being, like the flowers. Grateful for being alive.

Go home and see the first sliver of a new moon over the roof top. Think it is time to make a new start in some area of life. A good idea seems to be 'seeing the ultimate equality of praise and blame.' Open door of house onto a whole new beginning. Friends discussing book I was thinking about on my journey. Get excited. Remember to breath, slowly. Join in. Leave to cut up vegetables very slowly, while listening. We all decide to meditate together. Don't want to stop. The others go out. I hardly notice. Later need a cuddle. Have to wait. Slight anxiety. Stay in the now. Breathe. Say the name of Rhea, over and over again. Look at vase of flowers for an hour. Think about drawing it, but don't need to. Have cuddle later. Happy.

Things to do: Recognizing the Other
1. Think about people you know who might be seen as 'other'. Write down honestly all your stereotypes around them. Don't judge yourself. Then look to see if any of these are hidden aspects of yourself.

2. Write down everything you do for one whole day. First do this in relation to all the hierarchies that lurk below the surface or blatantly on top. Secondly notice when you are in the flow, living rhythmically, equalizing naturally. Thirdly see what stops it. What thoughts do you have that suddenly block the flow?

3. Try just being for an hour a day, doing absolutely nothing.

4. Write down all the synchronistic happenings in your life for a week.

REFERENCES

Chapter One.

1. Pamuk. O. (2006) Quoted in the Guardian. 28.10.06.

2. Goleman. D. (1996) *Emotional Intelligence*. Bloomsbury. London.

3. Csikszentmihalyc. M. (1990) Flow: *The Psychology of Optimal Experience*. Harper and Row. NY.

4. Heraclitus in the Fragments quoted in Khan.C. (1979) *The Art and Thought of Heraclitus*. Cambridge University Press. Cambridge.UK.

5. Whitehead. A.N. (1978) *Process and Reality*. The Free Press. NY.

6. Christ. C. (2003) *She Who Changes*. Palgrave. Macmillan. NY.

7. Lao Tsu. *Tao Te Ching*. Trans. Feng. G and English.J. 1973. Wildwood House. London.

8. Hegel. G. (1841) *Phenomenologie des Geistes*. Auflage. Berlin.

9. Engels. F. (1934) *Dialectics of Nature*. Progress Publishers. Moscow.

10. Capra. F. 1992) *The Turning Point*. Flamingo. Fontana. London.

11. Teish.L. (1988) *Jambalaya*. Harper Collins. NY.

12. Blake. W. (1982)Erdman. The Complete Poetry and Prose of William Blake. Berkeley and Los Angeles.

13. Perera. S. (1981) *Descent to the Goddess*. Inner City Books. Toronto.

14. Walker. B. (1983) *The Women's Encyclopedia of Myths and Secrets*. Harper and Row. San Francisco.

15. Mellart.J. (1975) *The Neolithic of the Near East*. Thames and Hudson. London. 1

16. Gimbutas. M. (1974) *The Goddesses and Gods of Old Europe*. Thames and Hudson. London.

17. Goodison. L. (1990) *Moving Heaven and Earth*. The Women's Press. London.

18. Eisler. R. (1987) *The Chalice and the Blade*. Harper and Row. San Francisco.

19. Baring.A. and Cashford.J. (1991) *The Myth of the Goddess*. Viking Arkana. London.

20. Fromm. E. (1977) *The Anatomy of Human Destructiveness*. Penguin. Harmondsworth. UK

21. Taylor. S. (2005) *The Fall*. O-Books. Ropely. UK.

22. Platon. N. (1966) *Crete*. Nagel Publishers. Geneva.

23. Sappho. Quoted on p.1. in *The Great Goddess*. (1982) Heresies Collective. NY.

24. Foucalt.M. (1980) *The Eye of Power*. P.70 *of Power and Knowledge*. Ed. Gordon.C. Pantheon Books. London.

25. Lacan. J. (1977) *Ecrits: A selection*. Trans. Sheridan. A. Tavistock publications. London.

Chapter Two.

1. Fuller. R. (2003) *Somebodies and Nobodies*. Consortium. NY.

2. Bachofen. J.J. (1967) *Myth, Religion and Mother Right*. (Trans. Manheim.R.) Princeton Univ. Press, Princeton.

3. Greer. G. (1999) *The Whole Woman*. Doubleday. London.

4. Goldstein. R. (2003) 20th.May. *Bush's Basket*. Article in The Village Voice. NY.

5. Reich. W. (1970) *The Mass Psychology of Fascism*. Penguin. Harmondsworth.

6. Fromm. E. (1941) *Escape from Freedom*. Rinehart and Winston. NY.

7. Phillips. A. (2002) *Equals*. Quote from page 8. Faber and Faber. London.

8. .Fanon. F. (1986) *Black Skin, White Masks*. Pluto Press. London.

9. James. O. (2007) *Affluenza*. Vermillion. London.

10. Fromm. E. See 6.

Chapter Three.

1. Brewer. E. (1894) *Brewer's Dictionary of Phrase and Fable*. Brewer. London.

2. Starhawk (1982) *Dreaming the Dark*. Beacon Press. Boston.
(1987) *Truth or Dare*. Harper Row. NY.
3. Reich. W. (1970) *Natural Work Democracy. In The Mass Psychology of Fascism*. See Ch.2. 5.
4. www.rhythmsofresistence.com
5. Chopra. D. (2005) Quote from Resurgence. Nov/Dec. No.233. P.9.

Chapter Four
1. www.peacecoalitionumbrella.org
2. See Ch. One.
3. Rowan. J. (1976). *Ordinary Ecstasy*. Routledge. London.
4.Grayham St. John (ed) (2003) *Rave Culture and Religion*. Routledge. London.
5. Grant. C. (1999) *Ring of Steel*. Macmillan Education. London.
6.Bakhtin. M. (1968) Quote from p.98. *Rabelais and His World*. Tras. Iwolsky.H. MIT Press Cambridge, Mass.
7. www.pflondon.com

Chapter Five
1.Wilber. K. (1981) Quote from p.7. *Up from Eden*. Routledge. London.
2. Neumann. E. (1955) (1963) *The Great Mother*. Princeton Univ. Press. Princeton.
3. Harris. R. (2006) Article in Feb. on www.integralworld.net
4. Thich Nhat Hanh (1991) *Peace Is Every Step*. Bantam Books. London.
5. Dass. R. (1971) *Be Here Now*. Crown Publishing. NY.
6. Tolle. E. (2005) *The Power of Now*. Hodder and Stroughton NY
7. Blake. W. (1982) Eternity. p.470 in Erdman. *The Complete Poetry and Prose of William Blake*. Berkeley and Los Angeles.
8. New Economic Foundation. (2006) The UK Interdependence Report. NEF. London.
9.Derrida. J. (1982) *Difference*. Ch. In The Margins of Philosophy.

Univ. Chicago Press. Chicago.

10. Rumi in Abdulla.R. (2000) Words of Paradise. Poems of Rumi. Frances Lincoln. London.

11. Tweedie.I. (1979) *The Chasm of Fire*. Quote from p.114. Element Books. Tisbury.UK.

12. Xenophanes Quoted in Guthrie. W.K.C. (1962) *A History of Greek Philosophy*. Cambridge Univ. Press. Cambridge.

13. See Platon and Taylor in Ch. 1.

Chapter Six

1. Lovelock. .J. (2007) *The Revenge of Gaia*. (1979) *Gaia*. Oxford Univ. Press. Oxford.

2. Watson. L. (1973) *Supernature*. Coronet Books. London.

3. Sahtouris. E. (1989) *Gaia. The Human Journey from Chaos to Cosmos*. Pocket Books. NY.

4. Green. B. (1999) *The Elegant Universe*. Quotes from p. 18 and p. 237. Vintage. London.

5. Narby. J. (1999) *The Cosmic Serpent*. Phoenix Orion Books. London.

6. Green. B. See Ch.1.

7. Capra. F. See Ch. 1.

8. Yeats. W.B. (1925) *A Vision*. Quotes from p.13 and p 89. Macmillan. NY.

9. Woolger. R. (1990) *Other Lives, Other Selves*. Aquarian Press. London.

10. Hillman. J. (1978) *The Myth of Analysis*. Quotes from p.284 and 287. Harper Torch Books. NY.

Chapter Seven

1. Jung.C. (1917)(1967) *Two Essays on Analytical Psychology*. In The Collected Works. Princeton Univ. Press. Princeton.

2. Hodge. J., Struckmann. K. and Trost. L. ((1975) Freudian quote on p.161. *Cultural Bases of Racism and Oppression*. Two Riders Press.

Berkeley, Calif.

3. Samuels. A. (1993) *The Political Psyche*. Routledge. London.

4. James. O. See Ch. 2.

5. Fromm. E. (1978) *To Have and To Be*. Jonathon Cape. London.

6. Rogers. C. (1967) *On Becoming a Person*. Constable. London.

7. Rowan. J. (1976) *Ordinary Ecstasy*. Quote from p.125. Routledge. London.

B O O K S

O books

O is a symbol of the world, of oneness and unity. In different cultures it also means the "eye", symbolizing knowledge and insight, and in Old English it means "place of love or home". O books explores the many paths of understanding which different traditions have developed down the ages, particularly those today that express respect for the planet and all of life.

For more information on the full list of over 300 titles please visit our website
www.O-books.net

SOME RECENT O BOOKS

Back to the Truth
5,000 years of Advaita
Dennis Waite

A wonderful book. Encyclopedic in nature, and destined to become a classic. **James Braha**

Absolutely brilliant...an ease of writing with a water-tight argument outlining the great universal truths. This book will become a modern classic. A milestone in the history of Advaita. **Paula Marvelly**
1905047614 500pp **£19.95 $29.95**

Beyond Photography
Encounters with orbs, angels and mysterious light forms
Katie Hall and John Pickering

The authors invite you to join them on a fascinating quest; a voyage of discovery into the nature of a phenomenon, manifestations of which are shown as being historical and global as well as contemporary and intently personal.

At journey's end you may find yourself a believer, a doubter or simply an intrigued wonderer... Whatever the outcome, the process of journeying is likely prove provocative and stimulating and - as with the mysterious images fleetingly captured by the authors' cameras - inspiring and potentially enlightening. **Brian Sibley**, author and broadcaster.
1905047908 272pp 50 b/w photos +8pp colour insert **£12.99 $24.95**

Don't Get MAD Get Wise
Why no one ever makes you angry, ever!
Mike George

There is a journey we all need to make, from anger, to peace, to forgiveness.
Anger always destroys, peace always restores, and forgiveness always
heals. This explains the journey, the steps you can take to make it happen
for you.
1905047827 160pp **£7.99 $14.95**

IF You Fall...
It's a new beginning
Karen Darke

*Karen Darke's story is about the indomitability of spirit, from one of life's
cruel vagaries of fortune to what is insight and inspiration. She has
overcome the limitations of paralysis and discovered a life of challenge and
adventure that many of us only dream about. It is all about the mind, the
spirit and the desire that some of us find, but which all of us possess.*
Joe Simpson, mountaineer and author of *Touching the Void*
1905047886 240pp **£9.99 $19.95**

Love, Healing and Happiness
Spiritual wisdom for a post-secular era
Larry Culliford

This will become a classic book on spirituality. It is immensely practical
and grounded. It mirrors the author's compassion and lays the foundation
for a higher understanding of human suffering and hope.
Reinhard Kowalski Consultant Clinical Psychologist
1905047916 304pp **£10.99 $19.95**

A Map to God
Awakening Spiritual Integrity
Susie Anthony

This describes an ancient hermetic pathway, representing a golden thread running through many traditions, which offers all we need to understand and do to actually become our best selves.
1846940443 260pp **£10.99 $21.95**

Punk Science
Inside the mind of God
Manjir Samanta-Laughton

Wow! Punk Science is an extraordinary journey from the microcosm of the atom to the macrocosm of the Universe and all stops in between. Manjir Samanta-Laughton's synthesis of cosmology and consciousness is sheer genius. It is elegant, simple and, as an added bonus, makes great reading.
Dr Bruce H. Lipton, author of *The Biology of Belief*
1905047932 320pp **£12.95 $22.95**

Rosslyn Revealed
A secret library in stone
Alan Butler

Rosslyn Revealed gets to the bottom of the mystery of the chapel featured in the Da Vinci Code. The results of a lifetime of careful research and study demonstrate that truth really is stranger than fiction; a library of philosophical ideas and mystery rites, that were heresy in their time, have been disguised in the extraordinarily elaborate stone carvings.
1905047924 260pp b/w + colour illustrations **£19.95 $29.95** cl